1910199

AMERICAN SYSTEM OF EDUCATION.

A

HAND-BOOK

OF

ANGLO-SAXON ROOT-WORDS.

IN THREE PARTS.

FIRST PART.
INSTRUCTIONS ABOUT ANGLO-SAXON ROOT-WORDS.

SECOND PART.
STUDIES IN ANGLO-SAXON ROOT-WORDS.

THIRD PART.
THE BEGINNINGS OF THE ROOT-WORDS

"The terms which first fall upon the ear of childhood."—EDIN. REV.

BY
A Literary Association.

LOWELL, MASS.:
FREDERICK PARKER, 21 APPLETON BLOCK.
NEW-YORK:
ALEXANDER MONTGOMERY, 17 SPRUCE STREET.
—
1853.

John A. Gray,
PRINTER AND STEREOTYPER,
95 & 97 Cliff, cor. Frankfort st.

A LETTER.

DR. WISDOM TO THE LITERARY ASSOCIATION.

GENTLEMEN:—This letter you owe to the request of one of your number. Some time ago Dr. —— called upon me, and in a very agreeable conference with him, I learned much about your plans. Among other things, he informed me that, you were about to bring out a Hand-Book of the Anglo-Saxon Root-words of our language. I suggested this to your Committee some time ago. It is part of your work.

You act prudently in confining the proposed Hand-Book *solely to the Anglo-Saxon root-words*. These words address the senses. They are easily understood, because the things which they represent are found in the walks of childhood. They appear *as distinct words* in our language, and retain much of their original form and meaning. Most of the *root-words of French and Classic origin* do not appear as distinct words in our language. Many of them have lost so much of their native form as to make it a difficult thing to trace them in the English language—too difficult, at least, for childhood. They cannot be presented at an early age with advantage; and when presented, I am of opinion, it should be in connection with their *derivatives*.

Your present work is *needed*. I have long felt this. The two Hand-Books already published, I am happy to learn, find an open and hopeful field. But it is too wide for them. The *farm*, gentlemen, you have cultivated, the *garden* you have just entered, wants your care also. The Hand-Book on the Anglo-Saxon Root-Words will meet the wants of children about eight years old—the wants of an important class of pupils.

The *division* of your course on Orthography may not so readily gain the approval of parents and teachers. It will gain it, however. It is based on some interesting facts in the constitution and life of children. They learn by EXCURSIONS. This is the character of the mind in early life: it is *excursive*. The bud, the blossom, and the fruitage of thought are seldom gathered at the same time—never in childhood.

The excursions of the young mind are SHORT. The journey whose end is not apprehended at the beginning fails to excite healthy emotions. The large text-book may fill the eye, but rest assured it will soon oppress the heart. Besides, there is a charm in the *little* for young minds, and the end of a book forms an agreeable break in study. It is a desirable resting-place in the journey, and such resting-places should not by any means be too far apart.

You will, I suppose, *omit the original word.* Excuse my seeming obtrusion upon your deliberations. To give it can answer no end. The child will not be able to understand it, or receive any advantage from it. In many cases he would not be able to pronounce it. The more advanced student would not expect to find it in an elementary work. What use is there, for instance, in saying that DECK is from *deckan,* and LOVE from *lufian?* Gentlemen, give the results of your learning, but not the details and show of it.

I would advise you to give at least, in the most of cases, the original *meaning* of the words. It will have a charm for the young mind. The child, I think, would be pleased to learn, for instance, that *queen* originally meant woman, *boor* a countryman, *husband* the house-band, and *wife* the one who weaves, because women did the weaving in olden times.

You will also give the *use* of the words. This cannot be wisely over-looked. Words are instruments of thought, and are of value to us only when we can use them. I would give their use in familiar questions and answers, the teacher using the word in a simple question, and the child answering with the same word. For instance: Teacher. Is *home* a dear place? Child. *Home* is a dear place. The principle of *imitation* is brought into use here, and by it, the child will be able to acquire a correct pronunciation and a ready use of words.

You will also retain the two chief features of your other Hand-Books—I mean the *arrangement* of words in the three classes of *nouns, adjectives,* and *verbs*—an arrangement that accords with the law of mind—and their *disposition* in groups under the things to which they relate. Such an arrangement and disposition amount to a discovery in education. They accord with the *growth* of mind. The word becomes a pleasing object of study, and the child, in going forth into the domain of language, finds himself still in company with the form and spirit of nature. Conducted in this way, education becomes a thing of pleasure as well as of duty. The word ceases to be an arbitrary sign; the word becomes a thing instinct with thought.

With much consideration,

I remain, gentlemen, yours truly,

LIONEL WISDOM.

AN INTERVIEW

BETWEEN

A TEACHER AND A MEMBER OF THE LITERARY ASSOCIATION.

THE following interview has something more than a local interest.

Saturday afternoon, January 14th, 1853. Mr. B——, a practical teacher, called upon me to make some inquiries about "The American System of Education."

"Sir," said he, "allow me to ask you some questions about the Hand-Books."

Member.—With pleasure. We are happy to talk about that which interests us.

Teacher.—True, Sir. I have seen your Hand-Book of Anglo-Saxon Orthography, and am much pleased with it. You have another Hand-Book!

Member.—Two, Sir. The Literary Association has three Hand-Books on English Orthography. In these books, the child is led over the whole domain of the English language. He follows its *historic growth* from the half-formed words, pa and ma, to the awful names of God and eternal things.

Teacher.—The growth of language! Sir, has language a growth!

Member.—An instructive and beautiful one. It is the body of thought, and, like our own bodies, grows into an organic whole. Every word is a member, and increases with the increase of every part. Besides this, it has a noble *historic growth.*

Teacher.—Explain it, if you please.

Member.—The English language, as we speak it, is not native to America nor England. It is a mixed language, having at least *five lingual elements.* All its parts were imported from the continent. Its native home is the far-famed Indus—the first seat of civilization.

Teacher.—Sir, this is new and somewhat surprising. I knew that our language contained Latin and Greek words. Proceed, Sir.

Member.—An illustration will explain what I have said. The English language is like an engrafted tree. The Anglo-Saxon is the *stock;* and the Gothic, Celtic, French, Latin and Greek are *engraftures.* History records their inoculation and growth.

Teacher.—This is what I have long wished to see. The Anglo-Saxon is the stock—the basis of the English language.

Member.—Yes. When it was introduced into England by the Angles and Saxons in 450 A.D., the Celtic was the language of the British islands. A few Latin words were mixed with it, the memorials of the Roman conquest. But the Celtic wasted away before the Saxon, as the Indian dialects in this country, have wasted away before the English; and the Saxon became the speech of those islands.

Teacher.—Very satisfactory. But how did the other elements come in?

Member.—In various ways. The Church, commerce, war, and learned men, introduced them. The old Saxon tongue was poor in some things, and borrowed *kindred words* from the Gothic; names of *places* from the Celtic; words belonging to *law, chivalry,* and *taste,* from the French; and *scientific* and *theological* terms from the Latin and Greek languages. In this way, it has become great—in this way, we propose to study it.

Teacher.—How, Sir! You excite my curiosity.

Member.—In its historic growth. We begin with the Anglo-Saxon, which is the stock. It is more than this. Let me take a new illustration. As the German, Celt, French, Italian, and Greek, become *Americanized* by coming among us, so their languages have been *Anglicized* by engrafture upon the Saxon.

Teacher.—I understand now. Allow me, Sir, to return to the Hand-Books. What do you propose to do in your first one?

Member.—To teach the Anglo-Saxon root-words. We begin with the *childhood* of the language. It becomes the young mind. What do we want with derivative words till we have learned their roots?

Teacher.—Just so. How do you present those words?

Member.—As nature teaches us. The child picks up whole words as he picks up whole flowers. He picks them up in connection with things. He goes forth, and *names* whatever he sees and feels. Then, he learns their *qualities,* and names them; and lastly, their *actions,* and names them also. Thus, father; dear father; dear father comes.

Teacher.—Your plan is simple. The child, too, studies things while he is studying words.

Member.—This is not all. The Anglo-Saxon words are nearly all *spelled* as they are *written.* So the ear and eye agree in studying them.

Teacher.—What do you propose in your second Hand-Book?

Member.—The *growth* of the Anglo-Saxon root-words—their derivatives. They are needed to meet the wants of the unfolding mind. By the use of *nine terminations, twenty-five suffixes,* and *eighteen prefixes,* we form some *five thousand* derivative words from the *one thousand root-words.* Language is a necessity of our nature, and is to be furnished as we need it.

Teacher.—I see your plan clearly, and admire it.

Member.—Every child should build up his own language as necessity requires it. Then, words would be ready weapons of the mind.

Teacher.—So they would. You said that the Association had a third Hand-Book. What do you propose in it?

Member.—To teach the engrafted parts of our language. This is done according to the plan laid down in the first and second *Hand-Books.*

Teacher.—Nothing can be more simple. The idea of learning our language in its historic growth is beautiful. How could it have been overlooked so long?

Member.—I know not. But these views only point out the framework of the system. *Instructions* introduce the child to the whole building.

Teacher.—In what, may I ask?

Member.—Instructions in the different *parts* of the English language; instructions also in the *growth of words* by terminations, suffixes, and prefixes.

Teacher.—These instructions are much needed.

Member.—I have not said all yet. The English language has a growth according to the LAWS OF MIND. This is pointed out in the arrangement of words as *nouns, adjectives,* and *verbs.* It has a SOCIAL GROWTH. This is seen in the engrafted elements. It has a growth according to REASON. The mind of man begins at home to unfold itself. From thence, it stretches forth to God. This is presented in the arrangement of words under the various things lying between home and heaven.

Teacher.—The subject grows in interest. I have been blind to its importance.

Member.—One thing more. The English language has an *etymology;* and this is the root of its orthography. Words are traced to their native languages. They are traced also to their natural sources in the organs of the body. The body is the wonderful instrument from which the soul evokes speech under the influence of the world.

Teacher.—Enough, enough, Sir! You have convinced me that I know little or nothing of my own language. The Hand-Books I shall study.

Member.—Sir, we have a noble language. Let us understand and teach it to the people.

TABLE OF CONTENTS.

First Part.

MATERIALS OF ANGLO-SAXON ROOT-WORDS.

	PAGE
INSTRUCTION I.—A WORD	13
INST. II.—THE SPOKEN WORD	13
INST. III.—HEARING	14
INST. IV.—SPEECH	14
INST. V.—THE ORGAN OF SPEECH	14
INST. VI.—WRITING	15
INST. VII.—THE WRITTEN WORD	15
INST. VIII.—SEEING	16
INST. IX.—TOUCH	16
INST. X.—THE HAND	16
INST. XI.—THE PICTURE	17
INST. XII.—THE SYMBOL	17
INST. XIV.—THE LETTER	17
INST. XV.—THE ALPHABET	18
INST. XVI.—LETTERS AND SOUNDS	19
INST. XVII.—A TABLE OF LETTERS AND SOUNDS	19
INST. XVIII.—THE ENGLISH WORD	20
INST. XIX.—SOURCES OF ENGLISH WORDS	21
INST. XX.—ANGLO-SAXON WORDS	22
INST. XXI.—ANGLO-SAXON ROOT-WORDS	23
INST. XXII.—SYLLABLES	23
INST. XXIII.—QUANTITY	23
INST. XXIV.—ACCENT	24
INST. XXV.—ARTICULATION	24
INST. XXVI.—ENUNCIATION	25

PAGE

INST. XXVII.—PRONUNCIATION 25
INST. XXVIII.—ORTHOEPY 25
INST. XXIX.—ORTHOGRAPHY 26
INST. XXX.—SPELLING 26
INST. XXXI.—PHONETIC SPELLING 27
INST. XXXII.—THE MEANING OF WORDS 27
INST. XXXIII.—THE USE OF WORDS 28
INST. XXXIV.—HOW WE USE WORDS 28
INST. XXXV.—INSTRUCTIONS ABOUT ANGLO-SAXON ROOT-WORDS 28

Second Part.

STUDIES IN ANGLO-SAXON ROOT-WORDS.

CHAPTER I.—STUDY 33
     Studies: The Study of Words—The Plan of Study—Model of
     the Plan of Study—Preparing a Study—Reciting a Study—
     Names of Things—Things.
CHAP. II.—HOME 39
     Studies: Outhouses—Kinds of Houses—Groups of Houses—
     Parts of a House—Household Stuff.
CHAP. III.—HOUSEHOLD 45
     Studies: Servants—Food—Clothing.
CHAP. IV.—MAN 48
     Studies: The Body of Man—The Head—The Chest—The Upper
     Limbs—The Lower Limbs—States of the Body—Diseases of
     the Body—The Senses.
CHAP. V.—THE SOUL 55
     Studies: The States of the Soul—Powers and Feelings of the
     Soul.
CHAP. VI.—BUSINESS 57
     Studies: Farming—Hunting and Fishing—Smithing—Manufac-
     turing — Warring — Buying and Selling — Teaching—Other
     Learned Callings—The State and Officers.
CHAP. VII.—TOOLS AND WORKS OF MAN 65
     Studies: Tools and Works of the Farmer—Tools and Works of
     the Hunter and Fisher—Tools and Works of the Housewright
     —Tools and Works of the Shipwright—Tools and Works of
     the Millwright—Tools and Works of the Smith—Tools and
     Works of the Weaver—Tools and Works of Manufacturers—

PAGE

Tools and Works of the Housewife—Tools and Works of the
Soldier—Tools and Works of Learned Business—Tools and
Works of Different Kinds of Business—Weights and Measures ·
—Numbers.

CHAP. VIII.—THE WORKS OF THE CREATOR 77
    Studies: The Earth—Bodies of Land—Bodies of Water—Mine-
ral Bodies of the Earth—Vegetable Bodies of the Earth—
Shrubs—Herbs - Grasses—Vegetables—Flowers — Some Productions of Plants—The Parts of Plants—Animal Bodies of
the Earth—Wild Animals—Water Animals—Reptiles—Insects
—Birds—Domestic Birds—Productions of Animals—Bodies in
the Heavens.

CHAP. IX.—PLACE AND TIME 92
    Studies: Places on the Earth and in the Heavens—Relative
Places—Larger Divisions of Time—Smaller Divisions of Time
—Relative Divisions of Time—Relations of Things and Events
in Place and Time—Connections of Things and Events in Place
and Time.

CHAP. X.—GOD 98
    Studies: God—Attributes of God—Relations of God to Man—
Abode of God.

CHAP. XI.—QUALITIES OF THINGS 100
    Studies: Qualities of Home—Qualities of Outhouses—Qualities
of Household Stuff—Qualities of the Household—Qualities of
Food—Qualities of Clothing—Qualities of Man—Qualities of the
Body of Man—Qualities of Parts of the Body of Man—Qualities
of the Soul of Man—Qualities of the Hunter and Hunting—
Qualities of the Farm and Farming—Qualities of War—Quali-
ties of the Manufacturer and Manufacturing—Qualities of the
Trader and Trading—Qualities of the Sailor and Sailor's Life—
Qualities of the Learned Professions—Qualities of Officers and
Offices—Qualities of the Works of Man—Qualities of the Works
of God—Qualities of Vegetable Bodies—Qualities of Animals—
Qualities of Light—Qualities of God.

CHAP. XII.—ACTIONS 111
    Studies: Actions of the Body of Man—Actions of the Hands of
Man—Actions of the Feet of Man—Actions of Man in the
Household—Actions of the Senses—Actions of the Soul of
Man—Actions of Food—Actions of Clothing in the House—

PAGE

Actions of the Housekeeper—Actions of the Householder—
Actions of the Hunter—Actions of the Fisher—Actions of the
Farmer—Actions of the Housewright—Actions of the Wheel-
wright—Actions of the Shipwright—Actions of the Millwright
-Actions of the Smith—Actions of the Weaver—Actions of the
Manufacturer—Actions of the Trader—Actions of the Soldier—
Actions of the Teacher—Actions of the Doctor—Actions of the
Artist—Actions of Minerals—Actions of Plants—Actions of
Animals—Actions of Wild Animals—Actions of Water Animals
—Actions of Birds—Actions of the Earth—Actions of Water
—Actions of the Heavens—Actions of God.

CHAP. XIII.—EVENTS... 137
    Studies : Events of the Household—Events in the Occupations
    of Man—Events in the Earth—Events in the Heavens—Events
    of God—Last Things.

Third Part.

THE BEGINNINGS OF WORDS.

CHAPTER I.—THE BEGINNINGS OF WORDS...........................145
    Studies : Words—The Organ of Speech—The Body and Words—
    The World and Words—The Soul and Words—The Beginnings
    of Words—Natural History of Words.

CHAP. II.—THE HUMAN BODY.....................................148
    Studies : The Organ of Speech—The Sense of Hearing—The
    Sense of Seeing—The Sense of Taste—The Sense of Smell—
    The Sense of Touch—The Hands—The Feet—The Muscles—
    The Organ of Breathing—The Covering of the Body.

CHAP. III.—MAN 153
    Studies : Man—Household—Society—Business of Man.

CHAP. IV.—THE WORLD...155
    Studies : The Earth—The Heavens—Form—Quantity—Place—
    Time—Relations of Things in Place and Time—Connections of
    Things in Place and Time.

CHAP. V.—THE SOUL AND GOD....................................157
    Studies : The Soul—God.

CHAP. VI.—THE END OF THE HAND-BOOK OF ANGLO-SAXON ROOT-WORDS. 158

HAND-BOOK

OF

ANGLO-SAXON ROOT-WORDS.

INSTRUCTION I.

A WORD.

THE lips move when we speak. Something passes from them, and falls upon the ear. It is called a word. *A word is that which passes from the lips.*

It has another meaning now. A WORD IS THE SIGN OF A THING. I speak, for instance, the word, *rose*, and it is a sign to you of what I mean. You *see* and *smell* that sweet flower.

What is a word? Give an instance.

INSTRUCTION II.

THE SPOKEN WORD.

SPEECH is a rich gift, and is shared alone by man. It is the power to think and feel aloud. It gives us the spoken word.

The spoken word is a sound used as the sign of a thing. If I say *book*, for instance, you hear a spoken word. It is a *sound*, and is used as the *sign* of a certain thing—a book.

What is a spoken word ?   Give an instance.

INSTRUCTION III.

HEARING.

- THE spoken word comes to the ear. Without hearing, it comes in vain. There is no sound. We could make none ourselves: we could not hear what others make.

Hearing is one of the five senses. *It gives us a knowledge of sounds.* As such, we should use it thoughtfully when we speak ourselves, or listen to others.

What is hearing ?   What do we learn from it ?

INSTRUCTION IV.

SPEECH.

SPEECH is a wonderful gift. It is shared alone by man, and gives us the spoken word. It does so when guided by the ear.

Speech is the power of making known what we wish in sounds. It breaks up the silence of the heart. We think and feel aloud.

What is speech ?

INSTRUCTION V.

THE ORGAN OF SPEECH.

THE word, *organ*, is the same as an instrument, or tool. The hand is an organ : so is the eye.

The organ of speech is that instrument by which the soul thinks and feels aloud. It is made up of the lungs, windpipe, larynx, tongue, teeth, palate, and lips.

What is the organ of speech? What are its parts?

INSTRUCTION VI.

WRITING.

THE child is not content to be able to speak what he thinks and feels. He wishes to write his thoughts. The pencil is used almost as soon as the tongue.

The word, *writing*, means smearing, as with wax. In olden times, people covered boards with wax, and wrote upon it with a steel pen. It means more now.

Writing is the art or practice of making letters with a pen or pencil. It gives us the written word.

What is writing? What did the word at first mean?

INSTRUCTION VII.

THE WRITTEN WORD.

THE spoken word passes away. We wish to keep it, and find out that sound can be written.

The written word is one or more letters or marks, used as the sign of a spoken word. If I write the word, *buzz*, for instance, I think of the sound, *buzz*, and then of the insect or whatever makes it.

What is a written word?

INSTRUCTION VIII.

SEEING.

THE written word is brought to the eye. Without seeing, it would be brought in vain.

Seeing is one of the five senses. *It gives us a knowledge of the color and forms of things.* As such, it is useful when we make written words, or read those made by others.

What is seeing ? What do we learn from it ?

INSTRUCTION IX.

TOUCH.

THE eye could never give us a written word, if left to itself. It needs the help of touch.

Touch is one of the five senses. Among many things which it gives us, *form* is only pointed out here. *Touch gives us form.*

What is touch ? What do we learn from it ?

INSTRUCTION X.

THE HAND.

THE eye and touch could not give us a written word without the hand. As the ear and speech needed the organ of speech to form a spoken word, so the eye and touch need the hand to form the written word.

The hand is the organ or instrument by which the soul gives shape to things, thinks and feels so as to be seen. By the hand, the written word has its shape, and becomes a sign of what we think or feel.

What is the hand ?

INSTRUCTION XI.

THE PICTURE.

THE picture was the first way in which men wrote their words. If they wished to write the words, *horse* and *man*, they drew a picture of them. So children begin to write.

A picture is a likeness of a thing drawn on a flat surface. The picture, as a kind of writing, meant two things: 1. It was the likeness of the thing. 2. It was the sign of its name.

What was the first kind of writing? What is a picture? What did it mean as a kind of writing?

INSTRUCTION XII.

THE SYMBOL.

THE picture was a slow way of writing a word. It took up too much time. Men wished to shorten the time and lessen the labor. The picture was changed into a symbol. Instead of drawing a picture of a siege, *a scaling-ladder* only was drawn: instead of drawing a king in royal dress, *an eye and sceptre* were drawn.

A symbol is a part, instrument or some likeness of a thing. *Feet in water* was the symbol of a fuller: an *arm with a whip* was the symbol of a charioteer, and a *fly* of impudence. The symbol, as a kind of writing, was a double sign: 1. A sign of the thing; 2. A sign of its name.

What is a symbol? What is it as a kind of writing?

INSTRUCTION XIV.

THE LETTER.

THE symbol, like the picture, was found to be a slow way of writing. It took up too much time. The Chinese shortened it. They wrote each word by making a certain mark, which became its sign.

This way was found not to be the best. Instead of writing EACH WORD by a mark, for then we would have to write and know EIGHTY THOUSAND MARKS to know all our language, we write only the SOUNDS of which words are made. In this case, we have only to learn the marks for FORTY SOUNDS, for these make up all the words in our language. These marks are called letters.

A letter is the sign of a sound of the human voice; as, a, b, c. When I see *a* or *o*, for instance, I think of the sound.

What is a letter?

WORDS, we have said, are made up of sounds. Thus, the word, *man,* is made up of the three sounds, *m, a, n.*

The sounds of which words are made, are written by letters. Thus, the sounds which make up the word, *go,* are written by the letters, *g* and *o.*

All the letters which mark the sounds of which all the words in a language are made up, are brought together and called an alphabet.

Alphabet is a word which we have borrowed from the Greeks. *It is the name of all the letters which we use in writing words.*

The letters of our alphabet are brought together in a certain order. It is as follows: *a, b, c, d, e, f, g, h, i, j, k, l, m, n, o, p, q, r, s, t, u, v, w, x, y, z.*

What is the alphabet

INSTRUCTION XVI.

LETTERS AND SOUNDS.

ALL the words which we use are spoken with FORTY SOUNDS and written with TWENTY-SIX LETTERS.

Some of these sounds are made by opening the mouth and forcing out the air. These are called vowels.

A vowel is simple voice; as, a, o. It is formed by opening the mouth:

Some of these sounds are double. These are called diphthongs.

A diphthong is the union of two vowel sounds: as, *oi* in boil.

Some of these sounds are made by joining parts of the organ of speech. They are called consonants.

A consonant is a jointed sound. It is formed by joining parts of the mouth together: as, the lips in sounding P; the tongue and teeth in sounding T.

What is a vowel! A diphthong! A consonant!

INSTRUCTION XVII.

A TABLE OF LETTERS AND SOUNDS.

THE *letters* and *sounds* may now be brought together in one view, under the heads of VOWELS, DIPHTHONGS and CONSONANTS. They should be studied with great care.

I. VOWEL SOUNDS.

1. *a* as in father.	7. *i* as in pin.
2. *a* as in fat.	8. *o* as in note.
3. *a* as in fate.	9. *o* as in not.
4. *a* or *aw* as in water, law.	10. *oo* as in fool.
5. *e* as in me.	11. *u* as in tube.
6. *e* as in met.	12. *u* as in tub.

II. DIPHTHONGS.

1. *ou* as in house.
2. *oi* as in boil.
3. *ew* as in new.
4. *i* as in bite.

III. CONSONANTS.

1. *w* as in woe.
2. *y* as in ye.
3. *l* as in low.
4. *m* as in man.
5. *n* as in not.
6. *r* as in ran.
7. *p* as in pan.
8. *b* as in bin.
9. *v* as in van.
10. *f* as in fan.
11. *t* as in tin.
12. *d* as in din.
13. *th* as in thin.
14. *th* as in thine.
15. *g* as in gun.
16. *k* as in kin.
17. *s* as in sin.
18. *sh* as in shine.
19. *z* as in zeal.
20. *z* (*zh*) as in azure.
21. *ch* as in church.
22. *j* as in jest.
23. *ng* as in sing.
24. *h* as in he.

In looking over this table, it will be seen that there are
TWELVE VOWELS, FOUR DIPHTHONGS, and TWENTY-FOUR
CONSONANTS. These are all the sounds which we hear in
speech. They make up all our words.

Name the vowels. The diphthongs. The consonants. How many of each?

INSTRUCTION XVIII.

THE ENGLISH WORD.

THE words which we speak and write, are called English
words. We call them so because we got them from the
English—a people who live in England.

The word, ENGLISH, was taken from the name of a tribe
of people, called ANGLES. This tribe came over from the

north of Germany and settled in what is now called England, in A. D. 450.

What is the name of the words we use ? What did the name, *English*, come from !

INSTRUCTION XIX

SOURCES OF ENGLISH WORDS.

THE words which we use, like the people of our country, have come to us from different sources.

We have borrowed words from all quarters.

We have borrowed from almost every language under heaven. Merchants and travellers have brought us words from all parts of the earth.

We have borrowed words from the *Danish*. Such are the words, *dwell, flap, flabby, gasp.*

We have borrowed from the *Swedish*. Such are the words, *hassock, lag.*

We have borrowed from the *Dutch*. Such are the words, *belong, blear, blush.*

We have borrowed from the *German*. Such are the words, *fresh, boy, booby.*

We have borrowed from the *Celtic*. Such are the words, *bun, bug, kick, creak.*

We have borrowed from the *French*. Such are the words, *bias, beef, bottle, search.*

We have borrowed largely from the *Latin*. Such are the words, *globe, solar, ruby, part.*

We have borrowed also from the *Greek*. Such are the words, *sphere, poultice, peg, pirate.*

We have borrowed from the *Spanish*. Such are the words, *caste, musquito.*

We have borrowed from the *Italian.* Such are the words, *solo, stanza, piano, piano-forte.*

We have borrowed from the *Hebrew.* Such are the words, *jubilee, cherubim.*

There is another source from which we have got a large part of our words—from the ANGLES and SAXONS, who settled in England A. D. 450. The words from this source form the *root* of our language.

Name the sources from whence we have borrowed words. What can you say of the Angles and Saxons !

INSTRUCTION XX.

ANGLO-SAXON WORDS.

THE name, *Anglo-Saxon,* is taken from the names of two German tribes, *Angles* and *Saxons,* who settled in England A. D. 450. Their language became the speech of England in A. D. 836. It is our mother-tongue. To make it richer, we have borrowed from time to time from other languages. Some of them are mentioned in the last Instruction.

The ANGLO-SAXON words number about TWENTY-THREE THOUSAND.

1. *They are the words of home.* Such are the names of *father, mother, son, daughter, child, home.*

2. *They are the words of the heart.* Such are the words, *love, hope, sorrow.*

3. *They are the words of every-day life.* Such are the words, *ox, farm, plough, husband, wife, house, hearth, cook, eat, sleep, walk.*

4. *They are the words of the senses.* Such are the names of objects which we know through the senses ; as, *sun, moon, fire, water.*

Whence is the name, Anglo-Saxon ! What can you say of Anglo-Saxon words !

INSTRUCTION XXI.

ANGLO-SAXON ROOT-WORDS.

IF we take the cluster of words, HOME, *homely, homeless, homelier, homeliest, homeliness,* the word, *home,* is the root of all the others. It is a root-word.

A root-word is one that gives rise to others. Thus, the root word, FATHER, gives rise to *fatherly, fatherless, unfatherly.*

We are about now to enter upon the study of root-words of Anglo-Saxon origin.

What is a root-word ! Give an instance.

INSTRUCTION XXII.

SYLLABLES.

THERE are many words which can be sounded at once. Such are the words, *son, child.* There are also many words which cannot be sounded at once. Such are the words, *father, mother.* They are broken into parts, called syllables; as, *fa-ther.*

A syllable is a word, or so much of one as can be sounded at once; as, *man, child-like.*

What is a syllable !

INSTRUCTION XXIII.

QUANTITY.

IF I sound the vowels, *a, e, i, o, u,* the voice is lengthened. If I sound the consonants, such as *k, t, d,* the voice is shortened. When I speak the word, *father,* the voice is long on the syllable, *fa,* and short on the syllable, *ther.* This is called quantity.

Quantity is length of voice as heard in letters and syllables.
It is long, or short, and is marked thus, ‿ —; as in cŏn-
sūme.

What is quantity! Give an instance of the *long* and *short* quantity of
letters and syllables. What are the marks of quantity!

INSTRUCTION XXIV.

ACCENT.

THE voice, in sounding words of more than one syllable,
changes its *force*. It is stronger on one than on another.
This is called accent.

Accent is force of voice on one or more syllables of a word. It
appears on the syllable, *ty*, in the word, tyrant. Its mark is ´,
as on the word, mínute.

What is accent !

INSTRUCTION XXV.

ARTICULATION.

WE sound all the letters and words by using the organ
of speech. This organ is divided intó three parts:

1. The part for breathing; as, the *lungs* and *wind-pipe*.
· 2. The part for voice , as, the *larynx, glottis*, and *epiglottis*.
3. The part for articulation, or jointing; as, the *tongue,
palate, teeth and lips*. In speaking words, these parts come
together, and this is called articulation.

*Articulation is the joining of parts of the organ of speech to
form the sounds which make words.* Thus, in sounding *t*, I
have to join the tip of my tongue and my upper gums.

Articulation should be a daily exercise. The child should
repeat the table of letters and sounds daily.

What are the parts of the organ of speech ! What is articulation !

INSTRUCTION XXVI.

ENUNCIATION.

IF we notice the voice as we sound the letters of the alphabet, we will see that it goes forth in different ways. It swells on o, glides on z, hisses on s, crushes on *ch*, and rings on N. This is called enunciation.

Enunciation is the way in which we give out the sounds of letters. It should be *clear, strong* and *distinct;* and form a daily exercise.

What is enunciation ? What should it be ?

INSTRUCTION XXVII.

PRONUNCIATION.

LETTERS are formed into words, and undergo some changes. A, for instance, has one sound in father, and another in fate. TH is sharp in thin, but flat in thine. To mark these changes, and give the true sounds of letters in words, is the part of pronunciation.

Pronunciation is the giving of the right sounds to letters in words, and accents to syllables. Thus, *neither* should be pronounced as if written *nee'ther*, and not as if written nayther, or neethér.

What is pronunciation ? What two things belong to it ?

INSTRUCTION XXVIII.

ORTHOEPY.

THE spoken word comes to the ear. It is a sound, and can be studied. The branch of knowledge that tells us all about it, is called orthoëpy.

2

Orthoëpy comes from two Greek words, and means *correct speaking*. It teaches us the spoken word—its sounds, syllables, quantity and accent.

What is orthoëpy? What does it teach? What belongs to it?

INSTRUCTION XXIX.

ORTHOGRAPHY.

THE written word is seen by the eye. It has form and parts, and can be studied. The branch of knowledge that tells us all about it, is called orthography.

Orthography comes from two Greek words, and means *correct writing*. It teaches us the written word—its letters, syllables, quantity and accent.

What is orthography? What does it teach? What belongs to it?

INSTRUCTION XXX.

SPELLING.

WE cannot write words unless we know the *sounds* that make them, and the *letters* which stand for these sounds. I hear, for instance, the word, *child*. How shall I be able to write it? By learning that it is made up of the sounds, – – –; and that these sounds are written by the letters, *ch, i, l, d.* This is spelling.

Spelling is naming the sounds that make a word, or writing the letters that stand for these sounds. Thus, I spell the word, *thin*, by naming the sounds, – – –, or writing the letters, *th, i, n.* Writing is the only sure way of learning to spell.

What is spelling? How many ways can you spell? Which is the better way?

INSTRUCTION XXXI.

PHONETIC SPELLING.

THE sounds given to the letters in the alphabet are not the sounds which they have in words. The letter, H, for instance, is called *aitch*, in the alphabet, and never has this sound in words. Its true sound is *heh;* as in he. This is very troublesome to children in spelling. Thus, we spell the word, *hat*, aitch, ā, te, and pronounce it, *hat.*

Phonetic spelling does away with this trouble. *It gives the true sound to each letter*—the sound which it has in the word. Thus, we spell in this way, the word, *church*, cheh, ŭ, er, cheh—church.

What is phonetic spelling? Give an instance.

INSTRUCTION XXXII.

THE MEANING OF WORDS.

WORDS are signs of things, and have a meaning. This must be known, or words are of little use to us. I have, for instance, the word, *deck*. How shall I use it? Its meaning will be my guide. *Deck* means to dress or adorn. The child *decks* her head with flowers.

The meaning of a word is what it stands for. It is best learned by seeing or feeling the thing. Thus, the word, *tooth-ache*, stands for a pain in a tooth. I know its meaning when I feel that pain.

No word should be allowed to find its way into the mind without its meaning.

What is the meaning of a word? How is it best learned?

INSTRUCTION XXXIII.

THE USE OF WORDS.

WORDS are a kind of tools. By them, we think and give shape to what we think. By words, we make known our thoughts and feelings. This is their use.

The use of a word is the employing it to stand for what it was made to stand for. Thus, we all have feelings. One of these is named by the word, *like*, and another by the word, *love.* I use these words, when I employ them to stand for the feelings, *like* and *love;* as, when I say, I *like* my books and *love* my parents.

No word should be allowed to find its way into the mind without a knowledge of its use.

What is the use of a word? How do we use words?

INSTRUCTION XXXIV.

HOW WE USE WORDS.

WORDS, as you have learned, are the weapons or tools of the mind. It uses them to tell what it thinks and feels. It can do so only in sentences.

A sentence is two or more words by which we say something of something. Thus, My mother is sick, is a sentence. It says something of something.

In the use of words, we use, in this book, two kinds of sentences. The teacher uses an *interrogative* one; and the child a *declarative* one.

An interrogative sentence is two or more words by which we ask something about something. Thus, Is home dear?

A declarative sentence is two or more words by which we say something of something. Thus, Home is dear.

What is a sentence ! How many kinds used in this book ! What is an interrogative sentence ! A declarative one !

INSTRUCTION XXXV.

INSTRUCTIONS ABOUT ANGLO-SAXON ROOT-WORDS.

THE end of the first part is reached. Here we may pause, and look back upon our course. We have learned many things by the way. We have learned all that is useful to us at present about the Ango-Saxon root-words of our language.

We are now ready to begin their study, and learn how to spell, define and use above ONE THOUSAND of the choicest words in our language—the words of home, of the heart, of the senses, of childhood and of daily life.

What have we learned up to this place ! What are we now ready to begin !

SECOND PART.

STUDIES IN ANGLO-SAXON ROOT-WORDS.

STUDIES

IN

ANGLO-SAXON ROOT-WORDS.

CHAPTER I.

STUDIES IN ANGLO-SAXON ROOT-WORDS.

THE study of words may be made a very pleasing one Words are wonderful things. Some of them are TALES, and some of them are HISTORIES. The Anglo-Saxon rootwords, which we are now going to study, are dear ones. They are signs of many sweet things about home and the heart.

FIRST STUDY.

STUDY.

THERE is no growth in knowledge without study. Without it, there is nothing learned well.

Study is fixing the mind on what we wish to know, and learning all we can about it.

In this way, we study trees and animals; in this way, we study our pains, hopes and sorrows. In the same way, we are to study words.

What is study?

2*

SECOND STUDY.

THE STUDY OF WORDS.

THERE are about ONE THOUSAND WORDS in this little book; and these are all to be studied. Their study is not hard. If you know how to study *one*, you will find it an easy thing to study all the others. An instance follows:

If the written word, *manly*, is to be studied, we fix the mind upon it through the sense of *sight*, and find out its *letters, syllables, accent, quantity, meaning* and *use*. Thus, *manly*, is composed of the letters, *m, a, n, l, y;* the syllables, *man, ly;* has the accent on *mán;* the syllable man is short, and ly is *long;* the word means *like man*, and may be used thus—Robert is a *manly* child. ·

If the spoken word is to be studied, we fix the mind upon it through the sense of *hearing*, and find out its *sounds, syllables, accent, quantity, meaning* and *use:* we also attend to *articulation, enunciation, pronunciation* and *spelling*. Thus, the word, *father*, is made up of the sounds, –, –, –, –, –; the syllables, fa, ther; has the accent on fă; fä is long and thĕr is short; the word means the male parent of man, and is used in this instance—*Father* is kind. In speaking it, we *join* the organ of speech in each sound, enunciate it clearly, and pronounce it thus—*fáthĕr*. We spell it thus—feh, ah, *fah*, theh, ĕ, er, *thĕr*, fahther.

There are some other things to be known in the study of words. They will come before us hereafter.

What is study! How do we study the written word! Give an instance. How do we study the spoken word! Give an instance.

THIRD STUDY.

THE PLAN OF STUDY.

A PLAN is a great help in every thing we wish to do. If we work without one, we will not work well.

A plan is a form, copy or model by which we are guided in our work.

The plan for the study of Anglo-Saxon *root-words*, is a very simple one.

1. The words are brought before the mind in GROUPS. Thus, *home, stead, homestead, house,* form a group.

2. Each group of words belongs to some THING. Thus, the group of words, *barn, shed, crib, rack* and *stall,* belong to outhouses. Outhouses are the thing.

3. The *names of things* are first given; then *the names of qualities;* and lastly, *the names of actions.* Thus, under HOME, we give the names of the *things,* home, stead, homestead, house; then the names of the *qualities,* sweet, dear; and lastly, the names of the actions, *draw, hallow.*

4. The meaning of each word is given. First is given the meaning of the word when it was made; as, *husband,* the house band or bond, binding the family together; and then the common meaning of the word; as, *husband,* a man wedded to a woman.

5. The *use* of each word is also given. The teacher asks a question, in which he uses the word, and thus gives a model to the child. The child turns this question into an answer, and gives the same *use* of the words. Thus:

Teacher. Is a barn a place for grain?

Child. A barn is a place for grain.

What is a plan? Go over the plan for the study of Anglo-Saxon root-words

FOURTH STUDY.

A MODEL OF THE PLAN OF STUDY.

THE child, in early life, imitates what he sees and hears. He learns from *models* better than from maxims or sayings.

This is true of the plan of study. We accordingly bring it before the mind in a model. We select HOME and its words.

THE MODEL.

HOME.

HOME is the dearest spot on earth. The heart turns to it, wherever we may be.

HOME, a cover; the place where one lives. *Teacher.*—Is *home* a dear place? *Child*—Home is a dear place.

STEAD, a stand; room or place. *Teacher.*—Shall I answer in your *stead?* *Child.*—You may answer in my stead.

HOMESTEAD, the place of home; one's abode. *Teacher.*—Do you like the old *homestead?* *Child.*—I do like the old homestead.

HOUSE, a closed place; a building to live in. *Teacher.*—Is your *house* large? *Child*—Our house is large.

In this model, every thing is done for the child. In the following studies, every thing is done, but ONE, *the answer* to each question, and this is easy. *The child has only to learn what is done, and be able to answer each question.*

Tell what is said about the model.

FIFTH STUDY.

PREPARING A STUDY.

THE study for the day is pointed out to the child. It may be HOME and its words. These are to be studied. He takes his seat and opens his book. *What is to be done?* WORDS ARE TO BE STUDIED.

STUDY.

Study is fixing the mind on what we wish to know, and learning all we can about it.

THE WRITTEN WORD.

In this case, the *written word* is the thing to be studied. The mind is fixed upon it through the sense of *sight*. What is it? *The written word is one or more letters used as a sign of the spoken word.* See Ins. VII.

THE SPOKEN WORD.

The written word becomes the spoken one, when we speak it. And what is this? *The spoken word is a sound of the human voice, used as the sign of a thing.* See Ins. II.

THE STEPS.

The steps in the study are easily marked.

1. The WRITTEN word. In studying this, the mind is fixed upon it through the sense of sight. We mark the *letters, syllables, accent, quantity, meaning* and *use* in the question of the teacher. See Ins. VIII.

2. The SPOKEN word. When we say the study, the written word becomes a spoken one. The mind is fixed upon it through the sense of hearing. We mark its *sounds, syllables, accent, quantity, meaning* and *use*. See Ins. III.

3. The *use of the word*. This is shown to the child in the question of the teacher, and is to be studied. The child learns what it means, and shapes an answer in the

same words. Thus he learns to use words, the weapons of the mind.

What is to be studied! What is study! The written word! Spoken word! The steps!

SIXTH STUDY.

RECITING THE STUDY.

THE child or class is called out to recite a study. It may be home. The recitation begins. The subject is home.

Teacher.—HOME. This is the subject of study. Robert, what do you know about it!

Child.—Home is the dearest spot on earth. The heart turns to it, wherever we may be.

Teacher.—HOME.

Child.—Home. Heh, o, em, e, (spelling it,) a cover; the place where one lives.

Teacher.—Is home a dear place !

Child.—Home is a dear place.

Thus, the recitation goes on till the study is ended. It is a pleasing talk, and cannot fail to bring light to the young mind.

How are the lessons to be said !

SEVENTH STUDY.

NAMES OF THINGS.

THINGS are about us every where. Their names are common and well known. They were the first words that we gathered up in childhood. What is a name?

A name is what we call any thing by. Tree is a name, for we call a certain thing by it.

The child first gathered up the names of things. It

learned the names, *pa*, *papa*, *ma*, *mamma*, *dog*, and could call them. So our knowledge of words began. So let our study of words begin—begin with the NAMES OF THINGS.

But with what things? Those of childhood. We begin with the names of the things of home, and go forth to the wide, wide world. We end with GOD.

What is a name? Do we begin to learn words with names?

EIGHTH STUDY.

THINGS.

THINGS, in some form or other, are ever with us. When we speak, or write, *words* are their signs.

Words and things go together. Words are of no use, unless we know the things for which they stand; and things have little interest for us, unless we have words to make known what we know and feel about them.

Things are greater than words. Words wait upon them. This being so, we wisely make them *points* of interest around which we gather groups of words. They should be made as full of interest as they can be, so that we may not soon forget the words which belong to them. The THING should be held up before the mind till its image is fixed upon the heart. Then its WORDS will abide in our memory.

What do you know about things and words?

CHAPTER II.

HOME.

HOME is the NURSERY of life. Here, our first hopes were born. And here, in scenes full of sweetness, we began to speak and gather up our first words. Here let us return and begin their study, for home is always dear.

> "How dear to this heart are the scenes of my childhood,
> When fond recollection recalls them to view;
> The orchard, the meadow, the deep-tangled wildwood,
> And every loved spot that my infancy knew!"
>
> S. WOODWORTH.

Repeat what is said about home.

NINTH STUDY.

HOME.

HOME is the dearest spot on eartn. The heart turns to it, wherever we may be.

> "Where'er I roam, whatever realms I see,
> My heart *untravelled* fondly turns to thee."   GOLDSMITH.

Repeat what is said about home.

HOME, a cover; the place where one lives.
Is *home* a dear place?
STEAD, a stand; place or room.
Is Robert in your *stead?*

HOMESTEAD, the place of home.
Do you love the old *homestead?*
HOUSE, a covering; a building to live in.
Is the *house* large?

TENTH STUDY.

OUTHOUSES.

OUTHOUSES are a very useful kind of buildings. They belong to every fine home in the country. Neat outhouses adorn a place.

What is said about outhouses?

Out, forth; on the outside.

Is the master of the house *out?*

OUTHOUSE, a building without the one in which we live.

Is the *outhouse* old?

BARN, a place for barley; a house for grain and cattle.

Is the *barn* new?

SHED, a shade or cover; an open place for cattle.

Is the *shed* low?

CRIB, that which catches; the manger or box out of which cattle feed.

Is the *crib* long?

RACK, something stretched; a frame from which cattle eat hay.

Was the *rack* burnt?

STALL, a stand; a stand for a horse or an ox.

Is the *stall* narrow?

ELEVENTH STUDY.

KINDS OF HOUSES.

THERE are many kinds of houses in which man dwells. They range from the Indian wigwam to the royal palace.

> "A straw-roofed cabin with a lowly wall,
> Mine is a fair and pillared hall,
> Where many an image of marble gleams,
> And the sunshine of picture for ever streams."   HEMANS.

Repeat what is said of kinds of houses.

HUT, a small cover; a small poor place to live in.

Have the Irish *huts?*

HOVEL, an open house, or cave; a rude house to live in.

Is a *hovel* low?

COT, something cut off for a cover; a very small, rude house.

Do poor people live in a *cot?*

COTTAGE, a cover to live in; a small house in which the poor live.

Are *cottages* pretty?

HALL, a tent; a large house where courts of justice meet; also a noble dwelling-house.

Is the *hall* a noble house?

CASTLE, a closed place of defense; a fortified house, or princely building.

Are there many *castles* in England?

CHURCH, the Lord's house; a house in which God is worshipped.

Is the *church* holy?

TWELFTH STUDY.

GROUPS OF HOUSES.

MAN is a social being. He likes to be near his fellow-man, and builds near him. Social homes arise, villages, towns and cities.

> "Sweet Auburn, loveliest village of the plain,
> Where health and plenty cheer the lab'ring swain."
>
> GOLDSMITH.

Repeat what is said about groups of houses.

HAMLET, a little house; a small number of houses together.
　Is the *hamlet* small?
TOWN, a fortified hill; a group of houses larger than a village.

Is the *town* noisy?
BOROUGH, a closed place; a town having its own rulers.
　Is the *borough* large?

THIRTEENTH STUDY.

PARTS OF A HOUSE.

THE house has many parts; and all its parts have their uses. The names of these form a fine group of words

> "Through that door
> Was shown:　　*　　*　　*　　*
> That deep descent leads to the dripping vaults;
> Leads to a covered bridge, the Bridge of Sighs;
> And, to that fatal closet at thy foot,
> An iron door. But let us to the roof;
> And when thou hast surveyed the sea, the land,
> Visit the narrow cells." ·　　　　ROGERS' ITALY.

Repeat what is said about parts of the house.

SIDE, drawn out; the long part of a thing.

Has a house two *sides?*

OUT, forth; on the outside.

Can you go *out?*

OUTSIDE, the side without a thing.

May the *outside* of a house be stone?

IN, inclosed; inside.

Were you *in* the house?

INSIDE, the side within a thing.

Is the *inside* of a house clean?

END, the point, or limit; the narrow part of a thing.

Has a house two *ends?*

DOOR, an opening; a passage into a house.

Is the *door* painted?

POST, set or firm; an upright stick of timber.

Is the *post* square?

DOOR-POST, the upright part of the door-frame.

Do you see the *door-post?*

SILL, that is laid down; the wood or stone under a door or window.

Is the *sill* of the window wet?

ROOM, place or space; a part of the space in a house.

Is the *room* low?

BED, a spread; a tick filled with hair, wool, straw or feathers, on which to sleep.

Is a feather *bed* soft?

BEDROOM, space for a spread; a room to sleep in.

Is your *bedroom* large?

KITCHEN, a cooking-room; a room used to cook in.

May a *kitchen* be small?

COURT, a circuit; an uncovered space before a house.

Do children play in the *court?*

HEARTH, earth; the pavement or stone on which the fire is made.

Does the fire burn on the *hearth?*

ROOF, stretched over; the cover of a house.

Is the *roof* of that house flat?

FLOOR, spread out; the bottom part of a house or room.

Is the *floor* wooden?

GATE, a gap or passage; a large door.

Is the *gate* new?

LATCH, a catch; a bar to fasten a door.

Is the *latch* made of iron?

FOURTEENTH STUDY.

HOUSEHOLD-STUFF.

A BUILDING in itself does not form a home. Furniture is also needed.

> "Yet I saw the idle loom
> Still in its place; his Sunday garment hung
> Upon the self-same nail; his very staff
> Stood undisturbed behind the door." WORDSWORTH.

Repeat what is said about household-stuff.

HOUSE, a covering; a building for storage or dwelling.

Do we live in a *house?*

HOLD, grasp; what is embraced or contained.

Is your *hold* firm?

HOUSEHOLD, those contained in a house; the persons who live in it.

Do those who live in a house make the *household?*

STUFF, that which fills; household articles.

Shall we keep useless *stuff?*

HOUSEHOLD-STUFF, the things in a house.

Are chairs *household-stuff?*

BED, a spread; that on which we sleep.

Are *beds* useful things?

BOLSTER, that which raises up; a cushion for the head.

Is the *bolster* soft?

PILLOW, a stuffing; a small cushion for the head.

Are *pillows* stuffed with feathers?

SHEET, a cloth; a linen or cotton under cover for a bed.

Are *sheets* made of muslin?

WASH, a flowing; a cleansing with water.

Did you see the *wash?*

STAND, a station; a place or frame on which any thing may be laid.

Is the *stand* small?

WASHSTAND, the frame or table at which one washes.

Is the *washstand* light?

BOWL, a hollow; a vessel to hold water in.

Is the *bowl* broken?

STOOL, a seat; a seat without a back.

Is the *stool* made of wood?

STOVE, a fixed place; that in which we make fire.

Do we burn fire in a *stove?*

PAN, spread out; a broad hollow vessel.

Is the milk *pan* new?

CRADLE, a rocking; the bed on which small children are rocked.

Does the *cradle* injure the head?

CROCK, a pot; an earthen vessel.

Is the *crock* made of earth?

DISH, something flat; a broad open vessel to eat off.

Are *dishes* easily broken?

FORK, a parted rod; that with which we lift our food.

Are *forks* made of silver?

KNIFE, that which nips; that with which we cut any thing.

Is the *knife* made of steel?

CUP, a bending; a small vessel out of which we drink.

Do we drink tea out of a *cup?*

TONGS, shafts; a tool of two shafts joined at one end.

Are the *tongs* made of iron?

CHAPTER III.

HOUSEHOLD.

A FURNISHED house always leads us to look for a household—a family bound together by love.

> "And oh, the atmosphere of home! how bright
> It floats around us when we sit together,
> Under a bower of vine in summer weather,
> Or round the hearth-stone on a winter's night!"
>
> PARK BENJAMIN.

Repeat what is said about the household.

FIFTEENTH STUDY.

HOUSEHOLD.

THERE are many dear names in the household—names of love.

> "He entered in his house—his home no more,
> For without hearts there is no home." BYRON.

Repeat what is said about the household.

HOUSEHOLD, the persons who live in a house.

Is the *household* large?

HUSBAND, the house band; a man joined to a woman by marriage.

Is a *husband* the head of the family?

WIFE, one who weaves; a woman joined to a man in marriage.

Does the *wife* love her husband?

CHILD, issue; a son or a daughter.

Is a good *child* loved?

FATHER, one who feeds; the male parent of man.

Do you love your *father*?

MOTHER, the source; the female parent of man.

Is a *mother* dear?

SON, light; the male child.

May a *son* be idle?

DAUGHTER, grace; the female child.

Is a good *daughter* a blessing?

BROTHER, brood; a male child having the same parents.

Is your *brother* kind?

SISTER, set; a female child having the same parents.

Should you love your *sister*?

BAIRN, born; a child.

Is the *bairn* good?

KIN, kind, or class; those connected with us by blood or marriage.

Should our *kin* be dear to us?

KINDRED, those of the same family-relations.

Do you love your *kindred?*

SIXTEENTH STUDY.

SERVANTS.

SERVANTS form a very useful class of men and women.

"From his sixth year, the boy of whom I speak,
In summer, tended cattle on the hills."   WORDSWORTH.

Repeat what is said about servants.

COOK, boiling; one who makes food ready.

Is a *cook* useful?

MAID, able; a female servant.

Is the chamber-*maid* young?

KITCHEN-MAID, the girl in the cooking-room; one who works in the kitchen.

Is the *kitchen-maid* sick?

HOUSE-MAID, the girl for the whole house; one who keeps a house clean.

Is the *house-maid* busy?

WASHER, one who washes.

Is the woman a good *washer?*

WOMAN, the source of man; the female of man.

Is *woman* kind?

WASHER-WOMAN, a woman who washes clothes.

Is the *washer-woman* poor?

HIRE, price; wages for work.

Do servants get *hire?*

HIRELING, a little paid man; one who works for wages.

Is a *hireling* honest?

PLOUGH, that which thrusts; a tool to turn up the ground.

Is the *plough* useful?

MAN, a form or shape; a male of the human race.

Is a *man* strong?

PLOUGHMAN, a man who guides a plough.

Should the *ploughman* be strong?

CAR, that which runs; a vehicle moved on wheels.

Is the *car* drawn by one horse?

CARMAN, a man who drives a car.

Are there many *carmen* in cities?

TEAM, offspring; yoked horses or oxen.

Is an ox *team* strong?

TEAMSTER, one who guides, or who drives a team.

Does the *teamster* work hard?

SHEEP, a well-known useful animal.

Are *sheep* clothed with wool?

HERD, one who keeps.

SHEPHERD, a sheep keeper; a man who t

Is th

FOOT, that which treads; the part of the body on which we stand.

Do you like a small *foot?*

FOOTMAN, a servant who waits on foot.

Did the *footman* open the door?

STEWARD, a place keeper; a man who manages house affairs.

Should the *steward* be faithful?

HENCHMAN, a serving man; one who serves another.

Should a *henchman* be true?

SEVENTEENTH STUDY.

FOOD.

ONE of the first cares of a household is food.

"Every moving thing that liveth shall be meat for you; even as the green herb have I given you all things."—BIBLE.

What is said of food?

FOOD, what feeds; that which we eat to keep up life.

What is *food?*

BREAD, a lump of food; a kind of food made from flour. .

What is *bread* made of?

BARM, what works or boils; yeast or leaven.

Is *barm* used to raise bread?

MEAT, what we eat; any kind of food; flesh of animals.

Is *meat* healthy?

DOUGH, a tough mass; leavened flour kneaded, but not baked.

Is bread made from *dough?*

LOAF, a shaped mass; a mass of dough baked.

Is the *loaf* large?

HAM, the thigh of a pig salted and smoked.

Do you like *ham?*

MILK, what is got by stroking; the white fluid from female animals.

Is *milk* used in tea?

BUTTER, what is made by striking; the oily substance taken from milk by churning.

Is *butter* made from milk?

CHEESE, drawn or curdled; the pressed curd of milk.

Do we make *cheese* from milk?

EIGHTEENTH STUDY.

CLOTHING.

CLOTHING, next to food, is an early care of the household.

"Loveliness
Needs not the foreign aid of ornament,
But is, when unadorned, adorned the most."

THOMSON.

What is said of clothing?

CLOTH, what covers; any thing made of wool, flax or cotton.

- Is *cloth* warm?

CLOTHES, covering for the body.

Are your *clothes* tidy?

CLOTHING, all kinds of garments, or coverings for the body.

Have you much *clothing?*

MANTLE, what shuts; a cloak, or loose covering for the body.

Is the *mantle* made of silk?

BELT, what is drawn round; a band worn round the waist.

Do you wear a *belt?*

CAP, end or point; a low cover for the head.

May the boy wear his new *cap?*

SLEEVE, the hand; that part of the dress which covers the arm.

Are long *sleeves* warmest?

TIPPET, the top; a garment for the neck.

Is the *tippet* made of fur?

HOOD, a head-cover; a covering for the head of a woman.

May a *hood* be thick?

HOSE, a heel-covering; a covering for the leg.

Are woollen *hose* warmest?

GLOVE, a cover; a cover for the hand.

Do *gloves* keep your hands warm?

SHOE, something put on; a covering for the foot.

Are *shoes* made of leather?

HAT, a cover or defense; a cover for the head.

Does the boy wear a *hat?*

SHROUD, what wraps; the dress of the dead.

Are the dead put in *shrouds?*

CHAPTER IV.

MAN.

THE house, food, clothing and furniture, are all little or nothing compared with man. He is the greatest study of life.

"The glory, jest and riddle of the world."   POPE.

What is said of man?

NINETEENTH STUDY.

MAN.

MAN was made in the image of God; but sin has taken away his beauty and holiness.

> "How poor, how rich, how abject, how august,
> How complicate, how wonderful is man!
> A beam ethereal, sullied and absorbed!
> Though sullied and dishonored, still divine!" YOUNG.

MAN, a form or shape; a male of the human race.

　Has *man* a soul?　.

WOMAN, source of man; a female of the human race.

　Can *woman* love?

FELLOW, one who follows; a companion of the same kind.

　Where is your *fellow*?

GAWK, a cuckoo; a poor simple person.

　Is a *gawk* foolish?

BOOR, a rustic, or farmer; a rude countryman.

　Were the Saxons *boors*?

SWAIN, a boy; a young farmer.

　Is the *swain* happy?

GUEST, one who goes out; a visitor from a distance.

　Should we welcome a *guest*?

HEATHEN, a dweller on the heath: one who does not know the true God.

　Shall the *heathen* be converted?

KNAVE, a boy, a youth; a rogue, or person who is not honest.

　Do you like a *knave*?

CHURL, a male or strong man; a rude ill-bred man.

　Do you like a *churl*?

NEIGHBOR, a near rustic or farmer; one who lives near another.

　Who is your *neighbor*?

TWENTIETH STUDY.

THE BODY OF MAN.

THE body is the habitation of the soul. The old Saxons called it the soul's house.

> "Sure 'tis a serious thing to die:
> In that dread moment how the frantic soul

3

Raves round the walls of her clay tenement,
Runs to each avenue, and shrieks for help."   BLAIR.

What is said of the body of man ?

BODY, that is fixed; the frame of an animal or man.
  Is the *body* wonderfully made ?
SKIN, a covering; the covering of the body.
  Should the *skin* be kept clean ?

FRAME, joined; the skeleton of bones.
  Is the *frame* of the body made of bones ?
FLESH, soft; the soft part of the body.
  Does *flesh* cover the bones ?

TWENTY-FIRST STUDY.

THE HEAD—THE CHIEF PART OF THE BODY.

THE head of man is the seat of the soul.

"Remove yon skull from out the scattered heaps!
Is that a temple where a god may dwell ?
Look on its broken arch, its ruined wall,
Its chambers desolate, and portals foul:
Yes, this was once ambition's airy hall,
The dome of thought, the palace of the soul!"   BYRON.

What is said of the head ?

HEAD, the top; the upper part of the body.
  Is the soul found in the *head* ?
LIP, border; the border of the mouth.
  Is your *lip* red ?
NOSE, a ridge; the ridge of the face.
  Is the *nose* the seat of smell ?
NOSTRIL, the nose-hole; the passage through the nose.
  Do we breathe through the *nostrils* ?
TOOTH, a shoot; a bony substance growing out of the jaw.
  Does the *tooth* ever ache ?

MOUTH, an outlet; the outlet of the voice.
  Is the sense of taste in the *mouth* ?
TONGUE, a point or projection; the instrument of speech and taste.
  Is the *tongue* the chief organ of taste ?
CHEEK, a side; the side of the face below the eyes.
  Is there a bone in the *cheek* ?
CHIN, an edge; the lower part of the face.
  Is Jane's *chin* small ?

BROW, a ridge; the ridge over the eye. Is the *brow* formed of short hairs?

EYE, a fount; the organ of tears and sight. Does the sense of sight reside in the *eye?*

NECK, the knob, or nape; the part of the body between the head and the chest. Is my *neck* short?

EAR, a shoot; the organ of hearing. Is the *ear* very delicate?

BRAIN, the fore part; the soft substance in the skull. Is the *brain* in the head?

THROAT, swallow; the front part of the neck. Is the *throat* in the neck?

NAPE, a knob; the high joint of the neck behind. Is the *nape* of the neck behind?

TWENTY-SECOND STUDY.

THE CHEST—THE MIDDLE PART OF THE BODY.

THE chest contains the lungs and the heart.

"How his great heart
Beats thick! his roomy chest by far too scant
To give the lungs full play."

BLAIR.

What is said of the chest?

CHEST, a trunk; that part of the body from the neck to the stomach. Is the *chest* the seat of the heart?

BREAST, a bunch or swelling; the fore part of the chest. Is there a bone in the *breast?*

BACK, a ridge; the hinder part of the chest. Should we turn our *back* to a person?

RIB, side border; a bone which forms part of the frame of the chest. Are there twenty-four *ribs?*

SIDE, drawn out; part where the ribs are. Which is your right *side?*

LUNGS, long; the organs of breathing, consisting of air cells. Are there two *lungs?*

BREATH, vapor; the air taken in and thrown out of the lungs.

HEART, strong; the vessel that holds the blood. Is blood carried away from the *heart* by arteries?

LIVER, weight; a large red organ which separates bile. Is the *liver* in the right side?

GALL, yellow; a bitter bottle-green fluid. Is the *gall* bitter?

BLOOD, that which flows; the red fluid that flows from the heart. Is *blood* conveyed to the heart by veins?

LOIN, leaning in; the side below the ribs. Do the *loins* lean inward?

TWENTY-THIRD STUDY.

THE UPPER LIMBS.

THE hand is a wonderful work. No tool in the world is so skilfully made.

"I rose up to open to my beloved; and my hands dropped with myrrh, and my fingers with sweet-smelling myrrh."—BIBLE.

What is said of the upper limbs?

LIMB, a branch; a branch of the body.
  Are there four *limbs?*
ARM, a joint; the limb reaching from the shoulder to the hand.
  How many *arms* have you?
SHOULDER, a shield; the joint connecting the arm and body.
  Is there a large bone in the *shoulder?*
ELBOW, the arm bow; the angle made by bending the arm.
  Does the *elbow* contain bones?
HAND, that which seizes; the end of the arm, palm and fingers.

Is the *hand* useful?
FINGER, that which takes; one of the extreme parts of the hand.
  Have you ten *fingers?*
THUMB, an inch; the short thick finger.
  Is the *thumb* shorter than the other fingers?
FIST, fast or firm; the closed hand.
  Can you knock with your *fist?*
KNUCKLE, a coupling; a joint of the finger.
  Do you rap with your *knuckles?*

TWENTY-FOURTH STUDY.

THE LOWER LIMBS.

THE lower limbs of the body are wisely framed for carrying us from place to place.

"Hold up my goings in thy paths, that my footsteps slip not."—BIBLE.

What is said of the lower limbs?

THIGH, thick; that part between the body and leg.

    Are both *thighs* alike?

HIP, lump; the fleshy part of the thigh.

    Is the *hip* formed by the thigh bone?

KNEE, a knob or bunch; the joint of the thigh and leg.

    Can the *knee* be broken?

STEP, stretch or distance; the space between the foot.

TOE, a sprout; one of the extreme parts of the foot.

    Are there ten *toes?*

SHIN, a splint; the round bone on the knee.

    Is the *shin* the largest bone in the leg?

ANKLE, a ball or clew; the joint between the leg and foot.

    Are there three bones in the *ankle?*

FOOT, that which treads; the lower end of the leg.

    Has the *foot* ten toes?

HEEL, a lump; the hind part of the foot.

    Where is the *heel?*

TWENTY-FIFTH STUDY.

STATES OF THE BODY.

THE body changes from work to rest, and from play to sleep.

> "All the world's a stage,
> And all the men and women merely players;
> They have their exits and their entrances."
>
>   SHAKSPEARE.

What is said of the states of the body?

WORK, exercise; labor or active use of strength.

    Is *work* a means of health?

PLAY, a bending; exercise for pleasure.

    Do you like *play?*

REST, a ceasing; repose from labor.

    Do we take *rest* at night?

SLEEP, loose; repose from the use of body and mind.

    Does *sleep* refresh us?

HEALTH, that is whole; a sound state of the body.

    Are you in good *health?*

STRENGTH, that is stretched; power of body.

    Has a sick person much *strength?*

TWENTY-SIXTH STUDY.

DISEASES OF THE BODY.

DISEASE follows the steps of health in this world.

"Far from his friends he strayed, recording thus
   The dear remembrance of his native fields
   To cheer the tedious night; while slow disease
   Preyed on his pining vitals."   BRUCE.

What is said of disease ?

SICK, loathing; touched with disease.
    Is it painful to be *sick?*
PAIN, a straining; an uneasy feeling.
    Have the sick many *pains?*
PANG, a torture; great pain or agony.
    Do *pangs* often trouble us ?
ACHE, a pressing; constant pain.
    Is man subject to *aches?*
AGUE, a shaking; a cold fit.
    Is *ague* common to many persons ?

BLAIN, a swelling; a sore on the skin.
    Did God send *blains* on Egypt?
PIMPLE, a little point; a little rising on the skin.
    Do *pimples* break out on the face ?
CROUP, a croaking; a disease of the throat.
    Are children troubled with the *croup?*

TWENTY-SEVENTH STUDY.

THE SENSES.

THE senses are the instruments of the soul.

"Even so the soul in this contracted state,
   Confined to these strait instruments of sense,
   More dull and narrowly doth operate;
   At this hole hears, the sight must ray from hence,
   Here tastes, there smells—
   She is one orb of sense, all eye, all airy ear."
                                DR. HENRY MORE.

Repeat what is said about the senses.

SMELL, warm; the sense by which odors are noticed.

Is the sense of *smell* found in the nose?

SMELLING, the sense by which we perceive odors.

Is *smelling* one of the five senses?

HEARING, a pointing the ear; the sense by which we perceive sounds.

Is *hearing* found in the ear?

SEEING, seeking; noticing by the eye.

Does the sense of *seeing* lie in the eye?

CHAPTER V.

THE SOUL.

MAN is more than a living creature. "And the Lord God formed man of the dust of the ground, and breathed into his nostrils the breath of life, and man became a living soul."

> "Life is real; life is earnest,
> And the grave is not its goal.
> Dust thou art, to dust returnest,
> Was not spoken of the soul." LONGFELLOW.

What is said of the soul?

TWENTY-EIGHTH STUDY.

THE SOUL.

THE soul is the chief glory of man.

> "O listen, man!
> A voice within us speaks the startling word,
> Man, thou shalt never die!" DARRA.

Repeat what is said of the soul.

SOUL, life; that part of man which thinks and acts.

Does the *soul* die?

MIND, possessing; that part of man which knows.

Should you fill your *mind* with knowledge?

HEART, strong; that part of man which feels.

Is the *heart* of man evil?

WILL, fixed, or set; that part of the mind by which we plan.

Does the *will* plan to do things?

TWENTY-NINTH STUDY.

STATES OF THE SOUL.

THE soul undergoes many changes and passes from one
state to another.　It is cheerful this moment, the next it is
gloomy and sad.

> "'Tis the great art of life to manage well
> The restless mind."　　　　　ARMSTRONG.

What is said of the states of the soul?

MOOD, having spirit; temper of the soul.
　　Should we live in a happy *mood?*

SIN, missing; departure from that which is good and right.
　　Does God hate *sin?*

BLISS, blithe; mirth of mind.
　　Do we hope for *bliss* in heaven?

THINKING, drawing out; using the power of mind in forming notions.
　　Are we always *thinking?*

THOUGHT, that is drawn out; that which is produced by thinking.
　　Have we all some *thought?*

FEELING, a pressing; noticing things by the senses.
　　Do all possess *feeling?*

WILLING, setting; choosing something.
　　Is the soul *willing?*

WISE, searching; knowing or having knowledge.
　　Is God a *wise* being?

DOM, doom or judgment; state or dominion.

WISDOM, state of reaching toward, or knowing; right use of knowledge.
　　Does *wisdom* come from God?

THIRTIETH STUDY.

POWERS AND FEELINGS OF THE SOUL.

THE soul of man is a thing of wonderful powers.　Many
feelings lodge within it.

> "By degrees the mind
> Feels her young nerves dilate; the plastic powers
> Labor for action: blind emotion heaves
> His bosom; and with loveliest frenzy caught,
> From earth to heaven he rolls his frenzied eye."
> 　　　　　AKENSIDE.

What is said of the powers of the soul?

FEELING, a pressing; that which we learn by the senses.

   Have all *feeling?*

SHAME, a blush; a feeling of guilt.

   Have you no *shame?*

PRIDE, adorned; great thoughts of oneself.

   Is *pride* sinful?

HATE, hot; great dislike.

   Is *hate* to a person wrong?

LOVE, a leaning; delight in any thing.

   Is *love* a feeling?

SORROW, sore or heavy; pain of mind for some loss.

   Has a mother many *sorrows?*

HOPE, a reaching forward; expectation of future good.

   Does *hope* cheer us?

FEAR, a bearing down; a painful feeling in view of future evil.

   Has the sinner many *fears?*

GLAD, lifted up; cheerful.

   Does hope make our hearts *glad?*

GLADNESS, a kind of delight.

   Does *gladness* ever beam upon us?

LUST, a longing; a longing desire.

   Should we gratify all *lusts?*

SMILE, melting; a cheerful play of the lips.

   Do you like to see a *smile?*

TEAR, a drop; a fluid that is seen in the eye, the sign of joy or grief.

   Can you dry up your *tears?*

BELIEF, leaving with; an assent of the mind to what is true.

   Is your *belief* strong?

WIT, mind or knowledge.

   Has he much *wit?*

LAUGH, loose; an expression of mirth.

   Do you like to hear a man *laugh?*

LAUGHTER, audible mirth.

   Can you make *laughter?*

FRIEND, freed one; one free to love and be loved.

   Are true *friends* often found?

SHIP, shape; state or office.

FRIENDSHIP, love between two or more persons.

   Is *friendship* sweet?

CHAPTER VI.

BUSINESS.

MAN can be studied best in the business of life. Work and rest alike show what he is.

> "Let us then be up and doing,
> With a heart for any fate;
> Still achieving, still pursuing,
> Learn to labor and to wait."   LONGFELLOW.

What is said of business?

3*

THIRTY-FIRST STUDY.

FARMING.

The care of the soil is a very old calling. "Abel was a keeper of sheep, and Cain was a tiller of the ground."

> "Oft did the harvest to the sickle yield,
> Their harrow oft the stubborn glebe had broke;
> How jocund did they drive their team a-field,
> How bowed the woods beneath their sturdy stroke."
>
> GRAY.

FARMING, getting bread; the business of tilling the land.

Is *farming* a healthy occupation?

FARM, bread; a tract of land tilled by one man.

Is the *farm* large?

THRESHING, beating, or treading; the act of beating out grain.

Is *threshing* hard work?

MOWING, a heaping; the act of cutting down grass.

Is *mowing* heavy work?

REAPING, cutting; the act of cutting grain with a sickle.

Is *reaping* light work?

PLOUGHING, thrusting; the act of turning up the ground in furrows.

Is *ploughing* a work of the farmer?

SOWING, swinging or scattering.

RAKING, reaching; the act of gathering hay or grain.

Is *raking* a work of the farmer?

SHEEP, a well-known and useful animal.

Are *sheep* gentle?

HERD, a keeper.

SHEPHERD, a sheep keeper; one who takes care of sheep.

Did the star at Christ's birth appear to *shepherds?*

LAND, cleared place; ground that is tilled.

Is *land* dear?

LORD, a bread giver; a master or ruler.

Is *lord* a title in England?

LANDLORD, a bread giver to those who hold his land; the owner of land or houses.

Should the *landlord* be kind?

THIRTY-SECOND STUDY.

HUNTING AND FISHING.

MAN, in a rude state of society, depends for support on fishing and hunting. Nimrod, we are told, was a mighty hunter.

> "There was an old hunter camped down by the rill,
> Who fished in this water, and shot on that hill;
> The forest for him had no danger or gloom,
> For all that he wanted was plenty of room." HOFFMAN.

Repeat what is said.

HUNTING, thrusting; the chase of wild animals.

Was *hunting* an early employment?

HUNTER, one who chases wild animals.

Are there many *hunters* at the west?

FISH, rapid or lively; an animal that lives in water.

FISHING, the practice of taking fish.

Is *fishing* pleasant?

FISHER, one who takes fish.

Does the *fisher* pass through dangers?

THIRTY-THIRD STUDY.

BUILDING.

MAN, in early life, shows a taste for building. The house, boat and carriage engage his care.

> "Cedar of Maine and Georgia pine
> Here together shall combine." LONGFELLOW.

Repeat what is said.

HOUSE, a covering; a building to live in.

Is your *house* made of brick?

WRIGHT, work; a workman.

Is the *wright* busy?

HOUSEWRIGHT, one who builds houses

Is the *housewright* useful?

MILL, that softens; a machine for grinding grain.

Have you ever seen a *mill?*

MILLWRIGHT, one who builds mills.

    Is the *millwright* needed in the country?

SHIP, shape; a vessel to move on water.

    Has a *ship* sails?

SHIPWRIGHT, one who builds ships.

Does the *shipwright* need much timber?

FRAME, joined; the timbers of a building joined together.

    Is the *frame* strong?

BOARD, broad; a piece of timber sawed thin.

    Have you ever seen a *board?*

THIRTY-FOURTH STUDY.

SMITHING.

THERE were workers in metal in the family of Lamech.

> "Week in, week out, from morn till night,
>   You can hear his bellows blow;
> You can hear him swing his heavy sledge
>   With measured beat and slow."   LONGFELLOW

Repeat what is said.

SMITHING, a striking; the practice of working in metals.

    Did *smithing* arise very early?

SMITH, a stroke; one who works in metals.

    Is a *smith* a mechanic?

BLACK, livid, or wan; dark, or without light.

    Is night *black?*

BLACKSMITH, one who works in iron.

    Does the *blacksmith* need a forge?

SILVER, a bright white metal.

    Is *silver* a useful metal?

SILVERSMITH, one who works in silver.

    Can the *silversmith* make spoons?

GOLD, bright yellow; a bright yellow metal.

    Are pencils made of gold?

GOLDSMITH, one who works in gold.

    Does the *goldsmith* beat out gold?

COPPER, named from Cyprus; a pale red colored metal.

    Are pennies made of *copper?*

COPPERSMITH, one who works in copper.

    Does the *coppersmith* make many of our vessels?

LOCK, shut; any thing that fastens.

    Has the door a *lock?*

LOCKSMITH, one who makes locks.

    Can the *locksmith* fit in a key?

THIRTY-FIFTH STUDY.

MANUFACTURING.

BARK of trees, fibres, leaves and other raw materials were wrought up into useful articles of clothing in the early ages of the world.

Repeat what is said.

WEAVING, moving back and forward; the practice of uniting thread into cloth.

Is *weaving* a very useful employment?

SPINNING, drawing out; the practice of twisting fibres into threads.

Is *spinning* little heeded now?

SHOE, covering; a covering for the foot.

Is a *shoe* made of leather?

MAKER, one who strains or strives; one who shapes any thing.

Do you know a *maker* of shoes?

SHOEMAKER, one who makes shoes.

Can the *shoemaker* make many kinds of shoes?

WATCH, guard or watch; an instrument that marks time.

Is a *watch* useful?

WATCHMAKER, one who makes watches.

Will the *watchmaker* mend your watch?

CLOCK, a click or stroke; an instrument that marks time by striking.

Does the *clock* stand on the mantel?

CLOCKMAKER, one who makes clocks.

BOOK, beech, beech bark; thoughts printed and bound.

Is a *book* made of paper?

BOOKMAKER, one who makes books.

Is a *bookmaker* called an author?

HAT, a cover, or defense; a high cover for the head.

Do you like a silk *hat*?

HATTER, one who makes hats.

Is the *hatter* a mechanic?

NAIL, claw; a pointed piece of metal.

Is the *nail* useful to the housewright?

NAILER, one who makes nails.

What does a *nailer* make?

TURNER, one who rounds; one who forms things with the lathe.

Does the *turner* make tops?

THIRTY-SIXTH STUDY.

WARRING.

WAR too soon became a calling of man. The arms turned against wild beasts, were pointed at the homes and lives of men.

" No solemn host goes trailing by
    The black-mouthed gun and staggering wain;
Men start not at the battle-cry:
    O, be it never heard again!"   BRYANT.

Repeat what is said.

WAR, a struggle; the practice of arms.
    Is *war* cruel?

SHOT, that is darted; a ball or bullet thrown from a gun.
    Is *shot* used in war?

SHOOTING, darting; the act of firing guns or arrows.
    Is *shooting* dangerous?

FOE, hated; an enemy, or one who hates us.
    Is the *foe* near?

FEUD, hate; a deadly quarrel.
    Should we take part in a *feud?*

FIEND, hated; a wicked foe.
    Is Satan a *fiend?*

FIGHT, strife or struggle; a struggle in arms.
    Do men *fight?*

THIRTY-SEVENTH STUDY.

BUYING AND SELLING.

As soon as man had more of any thing than he needed, he thought of its sale. Trade arose.

"Travelling merchants have done much in all ages to add to the comfort and knowledge of man."

What is said of buying and selling?

BUYING, possessing; the act of getting things by paying for them.
    Is the merchant *buying* many things?

WEIGHT, that bears down; the quantity of any thing found by weighing it.
    Is there a ton *weight* of butter?

SELLING, giving; giving any thing for a price.

SHOP, shape; a building in which goods are shaped or sold.
    Is the *shop* very large?

SHOPPING, going to shops; going to shops to buy goods.
    Do ladies go *shopping?*

MONGER, a trader; a dealer in any thing.
    Has the *monger* a stall?

FISH, rapid or lively; an animal that lives in water.
    Is *fish* good to eat?

FISHMONGER, one who deals in fish.

    Does the *fishmonger* go about the streets?

IRON, struck or beaten; a hard grayish and useful metal.

    Is *iron* more useful than gold?

IRONMONGER, a dealer in iron.

    Does an *ironmonger* deal in iron?

BOOT, amends, or more; profit, or something more.

    Is *boot* given in trading?

——

THIRTY-EIGHTH STUDY.

TEACHING.

IN the early ages of the world, parents taught their own children. Parents were both teachers and ministers.

What is said of teaching?

> "Early had he learned
> To reverence the volume that displays
> The mystery, the life which cannot die;
> But in the mountains did he feel his faith." WORDSWORTH.

TEACHING, leading or drawing; giving knowledge.

    Is *teaching* useful?

TEACHER, one who leads; one who gives knowledge.

    Is a *teacher* kind?

PRIEST, one who stands before others; one who waits at the altar.

    Did the *priest* wait on the dying man?

CANON, a reed or measure; a church law; also a minister in the church.

    Should we obey the *canon* of the church?

MONK, separate; a man who retires from the world to attend to religion.

    Do *monks* live in an abbey?

NUN, not up, or mature; a woman who retires from the world to attend to religion.

    Does the *nun* live in a convent?

LEARNING, giving or getting knowledge; gaining knowledge in any way.

    Is *learning* useful?

LEARNER, one who gets knowledge; a person who is getting knowledge.

    Is a child a *learner*?

THIRTY-NINTH STUDY.

OTHER LEARNED CALLINGS.

THE doctor, lawyer and author arose after the teacher.

"A placid stillness reigns,
Until the man of God, worthy the name,
Arise and read the anointed shepherd's lays."

Repeat what is said.

Law, set or laid; a rule of life.
Is the *law* good!
Lawyer, a law man; one who practises law.
Does the *lawyer* plead!
Healer, one who makes whole; one who cures diseases.
Is the doctor a *healer?*
Beadle, one who bids or orders; a crier in a court of law.

What does a *beadle* do!
Canon, a reed or measure; a kind of minister in the church.
Does the *canon* preach!
Bishop, an overseer; an overseer in the church.
Is the *bishop* an overseer!
Elder, more old; an officer in the church.
Should an *elder* be pious!

FORTIETH STUDY.

THE STATE AND OFFICERS.

Kingdoms were formed at an early age of the world.
Public men arose as officers.

"When freedom from the mountain height
Unfurled her standard to the air,
She tore the azure robe of night,
And set the stars of glory there."

Repeat what is said of the state.

King, able; the chief ruler in a nation.
Has the *king* supreme power!
Queen, a woman; a female ruler.
Does a *queen* rule in England!
Earl, noble; a nobleman of the third rank.
Does the *earl* serve the king!
Knight, a boy; a man of rank bearing arms.
Is the *knight* brave!

Yeoman, common; an officer in the king's house.
Will the *yeoman* wait upon the king!
Lord, bread giver; one having supreme power.
Has the *lord* a castle!
Sheriff, a shire holder; an officer who executes law in a county.
Is the *sheriff* faithful!

PROVOST, place before; the chief officer in a town or college.

Does the *provost* oversee things?

WATCH, awake, that wakes; a strict guard; a man set to keep any thing.

Does the *watch* go about the city at night?

WATCHMAN, one who guards a city by night.

Is the *watchman* up early?

CHAPTER VII.

TOOLS AND WORKS OF MAN.

BUSINESS calls for tools. The farmer needs his plough and spade; the smith needs his anvil and hammers.

"Earth's thousand tribes of living things
At art's command to him are given;
The village grows, the city springs,
And point their spires of faith to heaven."   SPRAGUE.

What is said of tools and works of man?

FORTY-FIRST STUDY.

TOOLS AND WORKS OF THE FARMER.

THE farmer has now a great many fine tools. In the early ages of the world they were few and very rude.

"The farmers crop their living from their crop,
And each man shares the blessing of their shares."
        WATSON.

Repeat what is said.

PLOUGH, that thrusts; an instrument to furrow land.

Does the farmer use a *plough* in spring?

SPADE, broad; an instrument to dig the ground.

Can the boy dig with a *spade?*

SHOVEL, pushing; a hollow instrument to throw up earth.

Does the farmer throw up earth with a *shovel?*

HOE, hack or hew; an instrument to cut weeds and loosen the earth.

Does the gardener use a *hoe?*

RAKE, reach or stretch; an instrument to gather grass together.

Can you use a *rake?*

SICKLE, that cuts; a curved tool to cut grain with.

   Does the reaper use a *sickle?*

SCYTHE, an axe; a tool for mowing grass.

   Does the mower use a *scythe?*

HAY, cut; cut and dried grass.

   Do horses eat *hay?*

CROP, a gathering; grain and fruits of the earth.

   Is there a large *crop* this year?

WHEAT, that is rubbed; a useful grain, from which flour is obtained.

   Is *wheat* a grain?

BARLEY, corn or grain; a grain something like wheat.

   Do you like *barley?*

BEAR, corn; a kind of barley.

   Does *bere* grow in Scotland?

HEAP, a mass or bundle; a pile, as of grain.

   Is the *heap* large?

OATS, eaten; a kind of grain used for cattle.

   Do horses eat *oats?*

RYE, rough; a grain like wheat, but not so good.

   Do we make flour from *rye?*

FLAX, drooping; a plant from which linen is made.

   Has *flax* a blue flower?

WHIP, a thrust or throw; an instrument for driving animals.

   Does the teamster use a *whip?*

FORTY-SECOND STUDY.

TOOLS AND WORKS OF THE HUNTER AND FISHER.

THE hunter and fisher at first had only the club, stone and rude spear. Now they have nets, traps, guns and harpoons.

> "The patient fisher takes his silent stand,
> Intent, his angle trembling in his hand;
> With looks unmoved he hopes the scaly breed,
> And eyes the dancing cork and bending reed."   POPE.

Repeat what is said.

BOW, bent; an instrument made of bent wood and a string.

   Does the hunter use a *bow?*

ARROW, a shoot or rod; a poisoned weapon shot with a bow.

   Did the *arrow* pierce the animal?

TRAP, that trips; an instrument that shuts with a spring.

Was the beaver caught in a *trap?*

SHOT, that is darted; a ball or bullet thrown from a gun.

   Is *shot* made of lead?

ROD, a sprout; a pole for fishing.

   Has the fisher a *rod?*

HOOK, that which snatches; a curved piece of metal.

Was the fish caught with a *hook?*

SEINE, a drag; a large net for taking fish.

Was the *seine* full of fish?

WEIR, an inclosure; a fence of sticks in a river to take fish.

Was the *weir* broken?

NET, a knot; an instrument made of twine woven together.

Are the fishermen mending their *nets?*

HANDLE, that which is seized; that part of a tool held in the hand.

Do we take a thing by the *handle?*

FORTY-THIRD STUDY.

TOOLS AND WORKS OF THE HOUSEWRIGHT.

THE house is one of the most needed of all the works of man.

> "All are architects of Fate,
> Working in these walls of Time;
> Some with massive deeds and great,
> Some with ornaments of rhyme."   LONGFELLOW.

AXE, what hacks; a tool to hew timber and cut wood.

Is the *axe* a good tool?

HAMMER, the beater; a tool to drive or draw nails.

Is the *hammer* made of iron?

SAW, what cuts; a tool with teeth to cut wood.

Does the carpenter use a *saw?*

AUGER, the borer; a tool to make large holes.

Can you bore a hole with an *auger?*

HOUSE, a covering; a place for man to live in.

Is the *house* large?

LADDER, a leader; a frame of wood joined by rounds.

Can you go up a *ladder?*

GATE, a passage; a large door into an inclosed place.

Is the *gate* broken?

BRIDGE, what bears; a building raised over a river.

Is the *bridge* strong?

STEEPLE, that goes up; the tower of a church ending in a point.

Is the *steeple* high?

TOWER, a pile; a kind of a house for defense.

Are there many *towers* in England?

BOX, what is close; a case of boards.

Is the *box* made of wood?

CHEST, a hamper; a kind of close box.

Is the *chest* large?

BIER, what bears; a frame to carry the dead on.

Did you ever see a *bier?*

FORTY-FOURTH STUDY.

TOOLS AND WORKS OF THE WHEELWRIGHT.

THE wheelwright builds for us the heavy farm wagon and the airy carriage. His skill adds much to our pleasure.

CART, what runs; a carriage with two wheels, drawn by one horse.

Is a *cart* a kind of carriage?

WAGON, a way or passage; a carriage with four wheels, drawn by one or more horses.

Has the *wagon* come?

DRAY, what is drawn; a low cart.

Is the *dray* used in cities?

BARROW, what carries; a kind of a carriage.

Is a *barrow* useful?

WHEEL, what turns; a round frame of wood for a wagon.

Has the *wheel* a rim?

WHEELBARROW, a frame or box with one wheel.

Have you ever seen a *wheelbarrow?*

HAND, what holds; the palm and the fingers.

Is the *hand* used in drawing?

HANDBARROW, a frame with handles carried by two men.

Is the *handbarrow* a carriage?

SLEDGE, what strikes; a frame moved on runners.

Is a *sledge* used to run on snow?

RIM, the end or edge; the border of a wheel.

Is the *rim* covered with iron?

SPOKE, a shoot; a rod of a wheel.

Is the *spoke* made of wood?

NAVE, thick; the thick piece in the centre of a wheel.

Is the *nave* made of wood?

FORTY-FIFTH STUDY.

TOOLS AND WORKS OF THE SHIPWRIGHT.

"IN the ship-yard stood the master,
With the model of the vessel,
That should laugh at all disaster,
And with wave and whirlwind wrestle."

LONGFELLOW.

SHIP, what is shaped; a large vessel made to float on water.

Did the Saxons call their *ships* keels?

HULL, an outer cover; the frame or body of a vessel.

Is the *hull* made of wood?

DECK, an overspread; the covering of a ship.

Is the *deck* made of plank?

HOLD, what contains; the hollow part of a ship.

Is the *hold* full of ballast?

KEEL, stretched out; the timber that extends from stem to stern of a ship.

Is the *keel* covered with copper?

STEM, set or fixed; the fore part of a ship.

Is the *stem* of the ship slender?

STERN, place; the hinder part of a ship.

Is the *stern* the hind part of a ship?

MAST, a stock; a round piece of timber on which sails are fastened.

Was the *mast* carried away during a storm?

BOAT, a bag; a bottle, or skin bag; an open vessel moved by oars.

OAR, over; an instrument to row boats.

Is a boat moved by *oars?*

BALLAST, a load; heavy matter placed in the hold of a ship.

Has the ship much *ballast?*

SAIL, what flies; a sheet made of coarse cloth.

Are ships moved by *sails?*

ROPE, what binds; a thick line of several twirls.

Do *ropes* fasten a boat to the pier?

WHARF, what is thrown out; a kind of harbor.

Has the vessel reached the *wharf?*

PIER, through; a raised bank or mole in a river.

Is the *pier* made of stone?

FORTY-SIXTH STUDY.

TOOLS AND WORKS OF THE MILLWRIGHT.

"THE dam is broke, the wheel is still,
And moss o'erlays the ruined mill;
No voice is heard, no form is seen,
Upon the lovely village green."

MILL, what is set or made; a machine for making flour, or the house in which this machine is kept.

Is corn ground in a *mill?*

DAM, what stops; a wall raised to keep in water.

Is the *dam* at the mill high?

WHEEL, what turns; a round frame of wood or iron.

Has the mill a *wheel?*

WATER, what flows; a common and useful fluid.

Is *water* common?

WATER-WHEEL, a wheel turned by water.

Is a *water-wheel* large?

BREAST, a swelling; the fore part of man, or any thing.

Is the *breast* the fore part?

BREAST-WHEEL, a wheel where the water falls on the middle.

What is a *breast-wheel?*

OVER, above; above in place.

Is the sky *over* the earth?

SHOT, throwing out; a shooting or casting.

OVERSHOT-WHEEL, a wheel where the water falls from above.

What is an *overshot-wheel?*

UNDER, lower in place.

Is the grass *under* the tree?

UNDERSHOT-WHEEL, a wheel where the water strikes below.

What is an *undershot-wheel?*

HOPPER, what hops or shakes; a wooden box through which grain passes into the mill.

Does grain pass through a *hopper?*

FORTY-SEVENTH STUDY.

TOOLS AND WORKS OF THE SMITH.

"HERE smokes his forge; he bares his sinewy arm,
And early strokes the sounding anvil warm;
Around his shop the steely sparkles flew,
As for the steed he shaped the bending shoe."   GAY.

ANVIL, that on which things are shaped; an iron block with a smooth face.

Is an *anvil* made of iron?

SLEDGE, what strikes; a large hammer.

Is a *sledge* made of iron?

TONGS, shoots; a tool of two shafts, joined at one end.

Are the *tongs* made of iron?

BELLOWS, swelling; an instrument to blow the fire.

Can you use the *bellows?*

WEDGE, a mass; a piece of iron thick at one end, and sloping to the other.

Does the smith use a *wedge?*

SHOE, a cover; a rim of iron nailed to the foot of a horse.

Is the *shoe* nailed on?

NAIL, a talon; a pointed piece of iron with a head.

Are *nails* made of iron?

HASP, a catch; a clasp that passes over a staple.

Is the *hasp* made of iron?

LOCK, what closes; an instrument to fasten doors.

Can you break a *lock?*

KEY, what shuts; an instrument to shut or open a lock.

Does the *key* fit the lock?

WARD, a guard; part of the inside of a lock.

Must the key fit the *ward?*

SPRING, what leaps; an elastic body.
Has a watch a *spring* ?

LATCH, what catches; a small piece of iron or wood for fastening a door.
Is there a *latch* on the stable door ?

PIN, what holds; a pointed instrument.
Are *pins* made of brass ?

LINCHPIN, a pin used to keep on the wheel.
Is the *linchpin* made of iron ?

FORTY-EIGHTH STUDY.

TOOLS AND WORKS OF THE WEAVER.

THE weaver weaves a flaxen web, but we are for ever weaving a web of thought.

> "Yes; Love is ever busy with his shuttle,
> Is ever weaving into life's dull warp
> Bright, gorgeous flowers, and scenes Arcadian."
>
> LONGFELLOW.

LOOM, what is used; a frame of wood for weaving.
Did Jacquard invent a *loom* ?

REED, a shoot; a weaver's tool.
Does the *reed* part the threads of the warp ?

SPINDLE, extended; the pin used in spinning-wheels.
Is the *spindle* made of iron ?

YARN, what is borne out; thread spun from wool or flax.
Do we knit with *yarn* ?

SILK, what is drawn out; the thread of silk-worms.
Does the silk-worm make us *silk* ?

WARP, what is bent; the thread that runs lengthwise.
Does the *warp* run lengthwise ?

WOOF, what is cast; the thread that runs across.
Does the *woof* run across the loom ?

WEB, what is woven; a cloth woven out of yarn.
Is life a *web* which all must weave ?

KNOT, a joining; the joining of threads or cords.
Is the *knot* tight ?

SLAIE, what strikes; a weaver's reed.
Is the *slaie* use in weaving ?

FORTY-NINTH STUDY.

TOOLS AND WORKS OF THE MANUFACTURER.

"THE king's daughter is all glorious within: her clothing is of wrought gold. She shall be brought unto the king in raiment of needle-work."

BIBLE.

GLASS, green; a hard clear substance made from ashes.
    Was *glass* made at first?
CLOTH, what covers; material made of wool, hair, or flax.
    Is *cloth* warm?
SILK, what is drawn out; a kind of cloth made from the thread of the silkworm.
    Is *silk* glossy?
SHOE, a cover; a cover for the foot.
    Is the *shoe* made of leather?
CAP, what is put on; a cover for the head of children.
    Is the *cap* made of cloth?
NEEDLE, something sharp; an instrument of steel, with an eye and point.

Can you sew with a *needle?*
PIN, what holds; an instrument of brass, with a head and point, used for fastening.
    Is the *pin* made of brass?
COMB, what shaves; a toothed instrument for fixing the hair.
    Is the *comb* made?
HOSE, a heel-cover; a cover for the leg.
    Are *hose* woven?
LEATHER, the prepared skin of animals.
    Are shoes made of *leather?*
LIQUOR, what flows; a fluid substance of any kind.
    Is wine a *liquor?*
FELT, what stuffs; a kind of cloth.
    Is *felt* used for wadding?

FIFTIETH STUDY.

TOOLS AND WORKS OF THE HOUSEWIFE.

"OH, pleasant is the welcome kiss
    When day's dull round is o'er,
And sweet the music of the step
    That meets us at the door."

DRAKE.

MEAL, broken smooth; the substance of grain ground.
    Is *meal* the flour of corn?

LOAF, a set mass; dough shaped and baked.
    Is the *loaf* large?

BREAD, a portion; a mass of kneaded dough baked.

Is *bread* the staff of life?

SIEVE, what lifts; a utensil for parting flour from bran.

Is the *sieve* made of wire?

KETTLE, a hollow vessel used to boil water in.

Is the *kettle* made of copper?

CHURN, what turns; a vessel in which butter is made from milk.

Have you ever seen a *churn*?

LADLE, what lays or puts; a utensil used for dipping out liquor.

Is the *ladle* used to lift soup?

STOVE, a place; an instrument to make fire in.

Is the *stove* made of iron?

OVEN, what heats; a place for baking in.

Do we bake bread in an *oven*?

FIRE, rushing or raging; heat made from wood or coal.

Do you like to see a bright *fire*?

BEETLE, what strikes; a wooden hammer.

Is a *beetle* used for pounding?

BELL, what sounds; a hollow vessel used to make sounds.

Can you ring the *bell*?

GONG, going? a utensil used for a bell.

Is the *gong* struck to make a sound?

KNIFE, what nips; that with which we cut our food.

Is the *knife* steel?

FORK, what is notched; that with which we lift the food to our mouths.

Is the *fork* silver?

FAN, what opens; an instrument by which air is moved.

Is the *fan* used to produce a wind?

BESOM, bound twigs; a brush used to sweep with.

Is the *besom* a useful article?

TOKEN, a mark; a mark of love and affection.

Is a present a *token* of love?

FIFTY-FIRST STUDY.

TOOLS AND WORKS OF THE SOLDIER.

"THEN shook the hills with thunder riven,
Then rushed the steeds to battle driven,
And, louder than the bolts of heaven,
    Far flashed the red artillery."   CAMPBELL.

SHIELD, a shoulder-cover; a broad piece of armor.

Is the *shield* worn now?

TARGET, what stops; a mark for gunners to fire at.

Do soldiers fire at a *target*?

SWORD, what thrusts; a weapon worn at the side.

Is the *sword* used in war?

SPEAR, what runs to a point; a long pointed weapon used in war.

Is the *spear* used by thrusting?

ARROW, a shoot; a weapon shot from a bow.

Is the *arrow* barbed?

ARMOR, what fits; a kind of dress worn for defense in battle.

Do knights wear *armor?*

SPUR, what is pointed; an instrument worn on the heel to prick the horse.

Is the *spur* much worn?

SLING, what is swung; an instrument to throw stones.

Did David use a *sling?*

SHOT, what is thrown; a weapon cast from a gun.

Is *shot* made of lead and iron?

BOW, what is bent; a bent piece of wood and a string.

Do the Indians use *bows?*

HELMET, what holds; a piece of armor for the head.

Is the *helmet* worn by soldiers?

TOWER, a pile; a kind of building, or part of one.

Are there *towers* on castles?

CASTLE, what defends; a house fortified against an enemy.

Are there *castles* in this country?

MOUND, a heap; a bank of earth or stone.

Have you ever seen a *mound?*

FIFTY-SECOND STUDY.

TOOLS AND WORKS OF LEARNED BUSINESS.

MUSIC is a noble work, and lifts the soul towards heaven.

" God sent his singers upon earth,
With songs of sadness and of mirth,
That they might touch the hearts of men,
And bring them back to heaven again."

LONGFELLOW.

HARP, that which is touched; a stringed instrument of music.

Did David play on the *harp?*

PIPE, that on which we pip, or pipe; a wind instrument of music.

Is the *pipe* a wind instrument?

PEN, a point; an instrument used to write with.

Is the *pen* made of steel?

DESK, what is flat; a raised stand to write at.

Do we write on *desks?*

SONG, what is strained; words sung in a musical way.

Is a *song* pleasing?

BOOK, beech-bark; the thoughts of a man printed and bound.

Are *books* useful?

WORD, what passes; the sign of a thing.

Is a *word* the sign of a thing?

CREED, that on which we rest; what one believes.

Has the Christian a *creed?*

SPEECH, what is thrust out; spoken words.

Is *speech* a gift from God?

FIFTY-THIRD STUDY.

TOOLS AND WORKS OF DIFFERENT KINDS OF BUSINESS.

"God made man perfect, but he has sought out many inventions."

BIBLE.

WATCH, a guard; an instrument to measure time.

Are some *watches* made of gold?

CLOCK, what clicks; a machine for measuring time.

Is a *clock* moved by weights?

SADDLE, that is set; a seat to be put on a horse's back.

Can you sit on a *saddle?*

AWL, a sting; a pointed tool used to make holes in leather.

Does the shoemaker use an *awl?*

LAST, drawn out; a form of the foot made of wood.

Is the *last* wooden?

KILN, a furnace; a large stove or oven.

Do we burn lime in a *kiln?*

ROAD, a way; an open way for travel.

Do people walk on the *road?*

PARK, what is kept; an inclosed place for pleasure.

Are there many trees in a *park?*

WELL, boiling up; a place dug to get water.

Is the *well* deep?

TIMBER, wood; wood prepared for building.

Do we cut down trees to make *timber?*

TOW, what is tossed; the broken and coarse part of flax.

Are mats made of *tow?*

TOLL, a part; a tax paid for some advantage.

Do we pay *toll* on the turnpike?

DITCH, what is dug; a trench made by digging.

Is the *ditch* used to drain land?

FIFTY-FOURTH STUDY.

WEIGHTS AND MEASURES.

"With what measure ye mete, it shall be measured to you again."

BIBLE.

FARTHING, the fourth; the fourth part of a penny.

Is a *farthing* a copper coin?

SCALE, a shell; the dish of a balance.

Has a balance two *scales?*

WEIGHT, heavy; the quantity of any thing found by weighing.

Do we buy sugar by *weight?*

POUND, weight; a standard weight of twelve or sixteen ounces.

Do we buy tea by the *pound?*

HUNDRED, a circuit; the number of ten times ten.

Is a *hundred* ten times ten !

TON, a cask; the weight of twenty hundred.

Is hay bought by the *ton ?*

GRAIN, a kernel; the weight of a kernel of wheat.

Was a *grain* of wheat used for a weight !

FOOT, what we step with; a measure of twelve inches.

Is the *foot* used for a measure !

SPAN, a stretch; the space from the end of the thumb to the end of the middle finger when extended.

Is the *span* used in measuring now !

YARD, a rod or shoot; a measure of three feet.

Is the *yard* used for measuring cloth !

FATHOM, a thread; a measure of six feet.

Is the *fathom* used at sea !

MONEY, coin or impress; stamped metal used in trade.

Have we copper, silver, and gold *money ?*

POUND, weight; the value of twenty shillings.

Is the *pound* a gold coin !

SHILLING, a shield-coin; the value of twelve pence.

Is a *shilling* a silver coin !

PENNY, money; the twelfth part of a shilling.

Is a *penny* a copper coin !

FIFTY-FIFTH STUDY.

NUMBERS.

"TRADITION tells us that the numbers, with which we count, came from the borders of the lovely vale of Cashmere."

ONE, a single thing; the sign of a single thing.

Is *one* a number !

TWO, one to one; one and one.

Is *two* twice one !

THREE, a throw; two and one.

Is *three* three times one !

FOUR, spread out; two and two.

Is *four* two times two !

FIVE, joined; four and one.

Is *five* four and one !

SIX, five and one.

Is *six* five and one !

SEVEN, full; six and one.

Are there *seven* days in the week !

EIGHT, seven and one.

Is *eight* seven and one !

NINE, eight and one.

Is *nine* eight and one !

TEN, two hands; nine and one.

Is *ten* twice five !

FIRST, what bears or leads; before in time or place.

Do you like to be *first ?*

SECOND, what follows; next after the first.

    Is *second* next after the first?

THIRD, next after the second.

    What is the *third?*

FOURTH, next after the third.

    What is the *fourth?*

FIFTH, next after the fourth.

    What is the *fifth?*

SIXTH, next after the fifth.

    What is the *sixth?*

SEVENTH, next after the sixth.

    What is the *seventh?*

EIGHTH, next after the seventh.

    What is the *eighth?*

NINTH, next after the eighth.

    What is the *ninth?*

TENTH, next after the ninth.

    What is the *tenth?*

CHAPTER VIII.

THE WORKS OF THE CREATOR.

"THE works of the Lord are great, sought out by all those who have pleasure therein."

> "The tall rock,
> The mountain and the deep and gloomy wood,
> Their colors and their forms were then to me
> An appetite, a feeling and a love."   WORDSWORTH.

FIFTY-SIXTH STUDY.

THE EARTH.

THE earth is the abode of plants, animals and man.

"Solitary savannahs opened in the depth of the woods, and far off a lovely stream was flowing away in silence, sometimes among venerable trees, and sometimes through natural meadows, crimson with blossoms." BRYANT.

EARTH, dust; the world in which we live.

    Is the *earth* round like a ball?

EARTH, the dust and mould on which we walk.

    Were we made out of the *earth?*

WATER, what flows; a useful and abundant fluid.

    Is *water* a fluid?

LAND, a clear place; the solid matter of our world.

    Do people live on the *land?*

SEA, a basin; a large body of water

    Do ships cross the *sea?*

FIFTY-SEVENTH STUDY.

BODIES OF LAND.

MANY divisions of land appear on the surface of the earth.

> "The hills
> Rock-ribbed, and ancient as the sun—the vales
> Stretching in pensive quietness between."   BRYANT.

HILL, what hides from view; a small rise of land.

Do you like to see a *hill?*

MOUNT, what goes up; a mass of earth higher than a hill.

Is the *mount* high?

PEAK, a point thrust out; the point of a hill or mound.

Are some *peaks* covered with snow?

RIDGE, stretched out; a range of hills or mounts.

Did you ever see a long *ridge* of hills?

CLIFF, what is cleft; a high steep rock.

Does the eagle build his nest on a high *cliff?*

BANK, a bench or seat; a pile of raised earth.

Does the *bank* defend them from the foe?

KNOLL, a little round hill.

Do sweet flowers grow on the *knoll?*

MEAD, wet; low wet land.

Is a *mead* low land?

MEADOW, low wet.land; a tract of low land.

Does grass grow in the *meadow?*

DELL, a cleft or division; a hollow place, between hills.

Would you like to live in a *dell?*

SHORE, cut off; the land bordering on the sea.

Do we go to the *shore* in summer?

ISLAND, water and land; a tract of land surrounded by water.

Is New-York on an *island?*

PIT, hollow place; a deep place in the earth.

Do miners go down in *pits* to get coal?

SWAMP, a sponge; a low land filled with water.

Is a *swamp* healthy?

SWARD, skin or rind; the grassy surface of land.

Does the green *sward* look cool in summer?

LEDGE, what is laid; a high row of rocks.

Can the goat walk on *ledges?*

DUST, dry fine earth.

Was man made from *dust?*

FIFTY-EIGHTH STUDY.

BODIES OF WATER.

THE sea is the great trading place of the world.

"The sea! the sea! the open sea!
The blue, the fresh, the ever free!
Without a mark, without a bound,
It runneth the earth's wide region round."

B. CORNWALL.

WATER, what flows; a fluid of great use and very abundant.
Do we drink *water*?

FOAM, what smokes; froth formed in water.
Is the river covered with *foam*?

SOUND, a swimming; a narrow sea or strait.
Is a *sound* very narrow?

BAY, what is bent; a part of the sea running up into the land.
Is a *bay* larger than a creek?

SHOAL, a crowd; a place where the water is not very deep.
Do ships often run into *shoals*?

STREAM, a flowing course; a flow of water.
Does the Indian paddle his canoe down the *stream*?

CREEK, a notch; a small bay or part of the sea running into the land.
Did the boat run into the *creek*?

HARBOR, an army station; a port for ships.
Has New-York a good *harbor*?

FIFTY-NINTH STUDY.

MINERAL BODIES OF THE EARTH.

CLAY, sand, rocks, water and air are all called mineral bodies.

"And the foundations of the wall of the city were garnished with all manner of precious stones."

BIBLE.

IRON, hard; a grayish, hard and useful metal.
Is *iron* made into steel?

TIN, sprinkled over or spread; a whitish soft metal.
Are many things in the household made of tin?

SILVER, a white brilliant metal.

   Are there mines of *silver* in Mexico?

GOLD, yellow; a yellow, heavy and precious metal.

   Is *gold* found in California?

LEAD, mass, heavy; a dull, whitish and soft metal.

   Are there many mines of *lead* in this country?

BRASS, bright; a metal made of copper and zinc.

   Is *brass* made of copper?

STEEL, what is fixed; iron and carbon together.

   Is *steel* made of iron?

SIXTIETH STUDY.

MINERAL BODIES OF THE EARTH, CONTINUED.

THERE are about *sixty* simple mineral bodies. These form the earth and all its plants and animals.

> "This vast assemblage of gigantic hills;
> Look at the craggy peaks which rise around,
> At the huge fragments of primeval rock,
> Those vestiges of elemental war."   LAUDSBOROUGH.

COAL, glowing; a black substance used for burning.

   Is *coal* a mineral?

SALT, biting; a substance used for seasoning.

   Is *salt* found in mines?

SAND, fine particles of stone.

   Is *sand* plenty?

FLINT, what flashes; a kind of stone, very hard and used in glass.

   Is *flint* very hard?

CLAY, sticky; oily earth.

   Is *clay* soft?

LOAM, soft; a mixture of sand and clay.

   Is *loam* a kind of earth?

BRIMSTONE, a burning stone; roll sulphur.

   Is *brimstone* yellow?

CHALK, close mass; a dull white earth

   Is *chalk* white and soft?

LIME, clammy; a kind of earth made by burning limestone.

   Is *lime* used in mortar?

STONE, firm; a hard mineral body.

   Is a *stone* hard?

LIMESTONE, a stone composed of carbon and lime.

   Is lime made from *limestone?*

SIXTY · FIRST STUDY.

VEGETABLE BODIES OF THE EARTH.

"It was autumn, and incessant
Piped the quails from shocks and sheaves,
And, like living coals, the apples
Burned among the withering leaves."   Longfellow.

TREES.

TREE, tall; a plant whose body is large and woody.

Has the *tree* a covering of leaves?

WILLOW, twig; a tree of a drooping form.

Do the branches of the *willow* droop?

SALLOW, pale; a kind of pale willow.

Is the *sallow* of a pale green?

OAK, strong; a hardy and noble tree, supplying fine timber.

Does the *oak* grow from an acorn?

MAPLE, cloth; a tree of a cone-like form.

Does the *maple* supply us maple sugar?

ASH, a grayish stately tree, affording good wood.

Does the *ash* give us good wood?

BIRCH, a tree with slender tough branches.

Does the *birch* make good rods?

BEECH, bark; a tall fine tree with silvery bark.

Were books made of *beech*-bark?

ELM, broad; a stately spreading tree.

Is the *elm* a noble tree?

LINDEN, a fine cone-like tree with rich flowers.

Is the *linden* a flowering tree?

HOLLY, hard; a glossy evergreen tree.

Does the *holly* bear red berries?

HAWTHORN, a hedge thorn; a shrub which bears the haw.

Is the *hawthorn* used for hedges?

FIR, point-bearing; a kind of pine, good for timber.

Is the *fir* good for timber?

HEMLOCK, border-plant; a kind of fir.

Is the *hemlock* an evergreen?

CHESTNUT, castle-nut; the tree which yields the chestnut.

Is the *chestnut* good wood?

YEW, a tree like the pine, often seen in church-yards.

Is the *yew* an evergreen?

APPLE, round fruit; the fruit of the apple.

Is the *apple* a good fruit?

APPLE-TREE, a tree that bears apples.

Is the *apple-tree* a native of Asia?

PEAR, the well-known fruit of the pyrus.

Is the *pear* a good fruit?

PEAR-TREE, the pyrus, or tree that produces the pear.

4*

Is the *pear-tree* large!
PLUM, a drupe, or stone fruit.
  Is the *plum* a stone fruit!

PLUM-TREE, the tree that yields the plum.
  Did the *plum-tree* come from Asia!

SIXTY-SECOND STUDY.

SHRUBS.

MANY of the shrubs which grow on our mountains bear flowers of the most rich and delicate colors.

"She sought the crystal brook, along whose banks,
With hazel and with honeysuckle fringed,
Lay the sweet winding way to school."   LAUDSBOROUGH.

SHRUB, rough; a low tree.
  Is the rose-bush a *shrub*!
THORN, a shrub having spines.
  Does the *thorn* bloom in the garden!
HAZEL, a cop; a shrub bearing a fine nut.
  Is the *hazel*-nut good to eat!
BRIER, rough; a shrub full of little thorns.
  Is the *brier* sweet!
BRAMBLE, prickly! any rough prickly shrub.
  Will *brambles* overrun the garden!
FURZE, thick; a thorny evergreen shrub, having yellow blossoms.
  Does the *furze* grow wild!

HEATH, clinging; a dry, brownish shrub.
  Is the *heath* used to make brooms!
WHORTLEBERRY, heart-berry; a shrub bearing a fine berry.
  Is the berry of the *whortleberry* good for food!
MISTLETOE, sticking; a shrub growing on the oak.
  Did the Saxons venerate the *mistletoe*!
IVY, up, climbing plant; a climbing shrub, growing on walls.
  Does the *ivy* climb the church wall!
MADDER, a plant used in dyeing.
  Is the *madder* used to dye red!

SIXTY-THIRD STUDY.

HERBS.

HERBS are useful to man. Some of them serve as food, others form his medicines.

"I have given every green herb for meat." BIBLE.

NETTLE, stinging; an herb whose prickles raise blisters.

Is the juice of the *nettle* good for burns?

HEMLOCK, border-plant; a poisonous plant.

Will the leaves of the *hemlock* poison?

FERN, a plant having its fruit on the back of the leaf.

Did you ever see *fern*?

RUE, bitter; a plant used in medicine.

Has the *rue* a bitter taste?

FENNEL, a plant having scented seeds

Is *fennel* pleasant to eat?

SIXTY-FOURTH STUDY.

GRASSES.

GRASSES, which include the different kinds of grain, are more useful to man than the trees and flowers.

"Let the earth bring forth grass." BIBLE.

GRASS, growing: plants that form the food of cattle.

Are *grasses* useful?

REED, a rod or shoot; grass with hollow-jointed stem.

Do *reeds* grow near wat· ?

CLOVER, club-grass; a plant with three leaves.

Is *clover* food for cattle?

RYE, rough; a useful grain.

Is *rye* easily raised?

BARLEY, bread-corn; a bearded grain.

Is *barley* used in making malt?

FLAX, drooping; a plant, the skin of which is made into thread.

Is linen made from *flax*?

HEMP, binding? a plant whose skin is used for cords.

Are the sails of a ship made from *hemp*?

SORREL, sour; a plant of an acid taste.

Can *sorrel* be eaten?

WHEAT, next to rice, the most useful grain.

Is flour made from *wheat*?

OAT, a plant yielding a grain for food.

Is meal made from *oat*?

SIXTY-FIFTH STUDY.

VEGETABLES.

VEGETABLES and fruit formed the food of man in the early ages of the world.

> "The moss his bed, the cave his humble cell,
> His food the fruits, his drink the crystal well."   PARNELL.

BEAN, a vetch; a plant with a straight stalk.

    Are *beans* used for food?

PEA, a climbing plant, yielding a pea good for food.

    Does the *pea* climb round a pole?

RADISH, ruddy; a plant whose root is eaten raw.

    Do you like the *radish?*

LEEK, long and pointed? a plant having a root like an onion.

Do *leeks* grow in the garden?

GARLIC, a dart; a plant having a root like an onion and an acid taste.

    Is *garlic* like onions?

PARSNIP, stone and knob; a plant with a spindle root, used for food

    Is the *parsnip* eaten?

TURNIP, round knob; a plant with flat or spindle-shaped root.

    Are *turnips* good for cattle?

SIXTY-SIXTH STUDY

FLOWERS.

FLOWERS are used to adorn the living and honor the dead.

> "In Eastern lands they talk in flowers,
> And they tell in a garland their loves and cares;
> Each blossom that blooms in their garden bowers,
> On its leaves a mystic language bears."   PERCIVAL.

DAISY, eye of day; a high, button-like flower.

    Is the *daisy* called the eye of day?

POPPY, pap; a showy plant, whose juice causes sleep.

    Was the *poppy* put in infants' food?

MALLOWS, soft; a soft, large-leafed plant.

Is the *mallows* leaf soft and large?

BLOSSOM, opened out; the flower of plants.

    Will the *blossoms* open in spring?

THISTLE, tearing; a prickly plant, with a showy head.

    Has the *thistle* prickles?

SIXTY-SEVENTH STUDY.

SOME PRODUCTIONS OF PLANTS.

PLANTS yield many things for the use and comfort of man

"The *cocoa's root*,
Which bears at once the cup, and milk, and fruit." BYRON.

APPLE, round fruit; the fruit of the apple-tree.
Is the *apple* a large fruit?
PEAR, a large fruit like the apple.
Is a *pear* shaped like a bell?
NUT, a hard lump; a fruit having a shell and kernel.
Does the *nut* contain a kernel?
BERRY, a grape stone; a pulpy fruit found on shrubs.
Do *berries* grow wild?
HAW, hedge; the berry of the thorn.
Is the *haw* a small red fruit?
SLOE, sour; the fruit of the wild plum.
Is the *sloe* purple?
ACORN, oak and grain; the nut of the oak.
Is the *acorn* small?

PLUM, solid; a fine stone fruit.
Is the *plum* of a dark color?
CORN, grain; the seed of such plants as wheat and rye.
Is bread made from *corn?*
TAR, wasting away; a thick, dark, sticky substance.
Has *tar* a dark color?
PITCH, thick; the thick juice of certain trees.
Is *pitch* useful to man?
GUM, lump cut off; the clear juice of some trees.
Does *gum* run from the peach-tree?
STARCH, stiff; a white substance, without smell or taste.
Is *starch* made from potatoes?

SIXTY-EIGHTH STUDY.

THE PARTS OF PLANTS.

PLANTS have many parts, all of which have their place and use. Wordsworth tells us about some of them, in the aged thorn.

"No leaves it has, no thorny points:
It is a mass of knotted joints."

STEM, firm, set; the body of a plant.
Is the *stem* always wood?
BOUGH, bent; the arm of a tree.
Is the *bough* very thick?
TWIG, what shoots; the smallest bough of a plant.
Do birds rest on the *twigs?*

WOOD, the solid part of a tree.
Is the tree cut down for its *wood?*
PITH, kernel; the spongy centre of a tree.
Does the *pith* often flow out?

BARK, what is peeled off; the outward covering of a tree.

Does the *bark* protect the tree?

SAP, soft; the juice of a tree.

Does *sap* flow in spring?

LEAF, light; the parts that shoot from the sides of the

Are *leaves* mostly green?

BLOSSOM, opened out; the flower of a plant.

Is the *blossom* of the apple-tree sweet?

SEED, sown; the part of a plant that produces new ones.

Does *seed* produce new plants?

KERNEL, a grain or nut; the part of a nut which may be eaten.

Is the *kernel* of the almond sweet?

SIXTY-NINTH STUDY.

ANIMAL BODIES OF THE EARTH.

·ANIMALS are teachers of mankind. They read us many a lesson.

> " The kitten sleeps upon the hearth,
> The crickets long have ceased their mirth;
> There's nothing stirring in the house,
> Save one *wee* hungry nibbling mouse.·
> Then, why so busy thou?"

OX, large; the male of the cow tribe.

Is the *ox* used in ploughing?

COW, what lows; a well known domestic animal, with cloven hoof.

Does the *cow* give milk?

HORSE, what rushes; a noble domestic animal, with feet not cloven.

Is the *horse* a native of Asia?

COLT, a young horse.

Is the *colt* frisky?

BULLOCK, what bellows; a little bull, or an ox.

Is the *bullock* a young bull?

SHEEP, a wether; a small animal useful for food and wool.

Has the *sheep* a covering of wool?

RAM, what thrusts; the male of the sheep.

Has the *ram* horns?

GOAT, what goes; an animal with hollow horns.

Does the *goat* give milk?

LAMB, what skips; a young sheep.

Do you like to see *lambs* play?

STUD, what stands; a fine horse for war.

Has the soldier a *stud?*

FLOCK, a crowd; a company as of sheep.

Does the shepherd tend his *flock?*

SWINE, what grunts; a thick-skinned animal, used for food.

Is a hog the same as *swine?*

Pig, a little one; the young of swine.

Has the *pig* a pen to live in?

Hound, fawning; a kind of dog used in hunting.

Is the *hound* a large dog?

Horn, a hard shoot; a hard substance growing on the heads of some animals.

Are combs made from *horn?*

Hoof, a horny substance on the feet of animals.

Is glue made from *hoofs?*

Hide, what is stripped off; the skin of an animal.

Are *hides* made into leather?

Marrow, fat; that which is found in bones.

Is *marrow* good for the hair?

SEVENTIETH STUDY.

WILD ANIMALS.

THE land is the abode of animals, some of which are useful to man. Many of them are wild and fierce.

> "The brindled catamount, that lies
> High in the boughs to catch his prey." BRYANT.

Elephant, chief or leader; an animal with a thick skin, and of great size.

Is the *elephant* a native of Asia?

Deer, roving or wild; an animal like the goat.

Is the meat of the *deer* used for food?

Doe, roving or wild; the female deer.

Was the *doe* killed?

Stag, firm or set; the male red deer.

Did the hunter chase the *stag?*

Hart, strong; a stag, or male deer.

Is the *hart* smaller than the stag?

Roe, a ray; the smallest deer.

Is the *roe* quick on foot?

Buck, what thursts; the male of the goat.

Does the *buck* jump far?

Elk, strong or large; a large deer.

Has the *elk* large horns?

Hare, what hears quickly; a small animal, with long ears.

Is the *hare* timid?

Fox, cunning; an animal like a dog.

Is the *fox* very cunning?

Bear, fierce; a large animal found in cold climates.

Is the *bear* wild?

Boar, rough; the wild hog.

Has the *boar* large teeth?

Otter, a small animal that lives in water.

Is the *otter* caught for his skin?

Rat, the gnawer; an animal like a mouse, but larger.

Do *rats* live in barns?

Mouse, what shuts up; a small animal which lives in houses.

Did the *mouse* eat the cheese?

Ape, quick; a four-handed animal, living in warm countries.

Does the *ape* climb?

SEVENTY-FIRST STUDY.

WATER ANIMALS.

The water on the surface of the earth teems with living creatures.

"And God created great whales, and every living creature that moveth, which the waters brought forth abundantly after their kind."   Bible.

Fish, lively; an animal with scales and fins.

Does the *fish* live in water?

Herring, army; a fish much used for food.

Has the *herring* many bones?

Trout, sharper; a fine fish, living in fresh and salt water.

Is the *trout* sweet?

Roach, red; a fish with shiny scales.

Does the *roach* live in fresh water?

Seal, set or placed; an animal having a head like a dog.

Is the *seal* found in cold countries?

Whale, the roller; a large animal, partly fish.

Does oil come from the *whale*?

Crab, scraping; a small animal having a crust-like shell.

Does the *crab* live in water?

Lobster, husky one; an animal like a crab.

Has the *lobster* many claws?

Clam, binding; a shell-fish used for food.

Has the *clam* a hard shell?

Fin, firm shoot; a limb of a fish used for swimming.

Is the *fin* very sharp?

Scale, a shell; a small crust which covers fish.

Are *scales* shiny?

SEVENTY-SECOND STUDY.

REPTILES.

The snake is loathed more than any thing on the earth. The memory of the fall of man, as written in the Bible, seems to live on from age to age.

"All turned with disgust from the scene;
  The worms they crept in, and the worms they crept out,
  And sported his eyes and his temples about." LEWIS.

SNAKE, creeping; a serpent of any kind.

Are *snakes* poisonous?

ADDER, poison serpent; a poisonous serpent of the viper class.

Is the bite of the *adder* poisonous?

SNAIL, crawling; a slimy, slow-creeping animal.

Is a *snail* black?

WORM, winding; a ringed animal, without feet.

Does the *worm* crawl?

LEECH, seizing; an animal like a worm, used to suck blood.

Are *leeches* found in lakes?

FROG, cracked in voice; a small four-footed animal that lives in water and land.

Does the *frog* live in water?

TOAD, a small animal like the frog.

Has the *toad* bright eyes?

TADPOLE, a young toad; a young frog.

Does the *tadpole* become a frog?

SEVENTY-THIRD STUDY.

INSECTS.

INSECTS please us. The butterfly is one of the joys of early life.

"I'd be a butterfly, born in a bower,
  Where roses, and lilies, and violets meet,
  Roving for ever from flower to flower,
  And kissing all buds that are pretty and sweet."

T. H. BAYLEY.

BEE, a small winged insect which makes honey.

Does the *bee* hum?

WASP, an insect like the bee.

Does the *wasp* sting?

HORNET, a kind of wasp.

Will the *hornet* build his nest?

FLY, moving by wings; a winged insect of various kinds.

Will the *fly* eat sugar?

GNAT, pointed insect; a small insect whose bite is sharp.

Do *gnats* bite in summer?

BEETLE, mallet; an insect with hard wings.

Has the *beetle* wings?

MIDGE, a kind of gnat.

Will the *midge* bite?

MOTH, what cuts; a winged insect which destroys cloth.

Does the *moth* eat cloth?

FLEA, a fly; a small black insect.

Is the *flea* red?

LOUSE, an insect that lives on the bodies of men.

Is the *louse* a parasite?

MITE, small; a very small insect which lives in cheese.

Is the *mite* very small?

EMMET, a small insect, as the ant.

Have you ever seen an *emmet?*

WEEVIL, a small insect of the beetle tribe.

Does the *weevil* injure grain?

SEVENTY-FOURTH STUDY.

BIRDS.

BIRDS teach us much that is wise and good.

"The *hen*, who from the chilly air
With pious wings protects her care,
And every fowl that flies at large,
Instructs me in a parent's charge."   GAY.

HAWK, a bird with crooked beak and feet.

Does the *hawk* live on flesh?

OWL, howling; a strange bird that flies at night.

Can the *owl* see in the dark?

KITE, a kind of hawk, swift in motion.

Does the *kite* move quickly?

RAVEN, the plunderer; a bird that lives on flesh.

Is the *raven* black?

CROW, the croaker; a large black bird.

Does the *crow* eat flesh?

ROOK, a bird like the crow that feeds on insects.

Is the *rook* like the crow?

LARK, the singer; a bird noted for its song.

Does the *lark* sing well?

THRUSH, the throat? a fine singing bird.

Is the *thrush* brown?

BLACK, pale; a pale or sallow color.

Is *black* the color of night?

BIRD, what is brought forth; a winged animal.

Can a *bird* fly?

BLACKBIRD, a kind of singing thrush.

Is the *blackbird* caught in nets?

SWALLOW, roof-bird; a small bird of passage.

Does the *swallow* fly quickly?

DOVE, cooing; a kind of pigeon.

Does the *dove* mourn?

CUCKOO, a wandering bird which sings well.

Is the *cuckoo* named from its note?

SWAN, white; a bird like the goose, with an arched neck.

BILL, a beak, or shoot; the beak of a bird.

Is the *bill* of a bird white?

WING, side; the limb of a bird used for flight.

CLAW, a foot-cleft; the sharp nail of a bird.

Is the *claw* of a bird sharp?

FINCH, fine, or gay; a singing bird.

Is the *finch* a small bird?

SEVENTY-FIFTH STUDY.

DOMESTIC BIRDS.

THE barn-yard has something to please and instruct us.

> "While the *cock*, with lively din,
> Scatters the rear of darkness thin,
> And to the stack, or the barn-door,
> Proudly struts his dames before." MILTON.

FOWL, flying animal; a winged animal.

Is the hen a *fowl*?

HEN, a cock; the female of any bird.

Does the *hen* love her chickens?

COCK, what shoots up; the male of birds.

Does the domestic *cock* crow?

CHICKEN, a small cock; the young of fowls.

Do you like to feed the *chicken*?

GOOSE, what cackles; a fowl that lives in water.

Is the *goose* a water fowl?

GANDER, the goose; a small goose.

Is the *gander* the male goose?

GOSLING, a little goose.

Is the *gosling* a young goose?

SEVENTY-SIXTH STUDY.

PRODUCTIONS OF ANIMALS.

THE song of the bird is the sweetest thing that animals give to man.

> "The *robin* warbled from his full clear note
> For hours, and wearied not." BRYANT.

MILK, what is got by stroking; a white fluid yielded by many animals.

Is *milk* good for children?

BUTTER, what is made from carrying milk in skin-bottles; an oily substance made from milk.

Is *butter* made by churning?

MEAT, what feeds; the flesh of animals.

Is *meat* good for food?

EGG, a body formed in female fowl.

Is the *egg* of the hen good for food?

WOOL, soft; the soft hair of sheep.

Is *wool* soft?

OIL, what kindles; a greasy substance.

Does *oil* burn readily?

HAIR, a thread-like growth on the skin.

Is the *hair* a vegetable body?

SEVENTY-SEVENTH STUDY.

BODIES IN THE HEAVENS.

THE sweet moon and the silent stars early please the young eye.

> "Nay! start not at that sparkling light;
> 'Tis but the moon that shines so bright
> On the window pane, bedropped with rain:
> Then, little darling! sleep again,
> And wake when it is day."

HEAVENS, lifted up or arched; the regions around the earth.

Are clouds in the *heavens?*

SUN, shining; that which lights the earth by day.

Is the *sun* bright?

MOON, the guider; that which lights the earth by night.

Does the *moon* shine at night?

STAR, the steerer as it guided sailors; a twinkling bright body in the heavens.

Can you see a *star?*

WELKIN, cloud; the arch of heaven as seen by the eye.

Is the *welkin* the same as the sky?

CHAPTER IX.

PLACE AND TIME.

PLACE and time are learned as we think of objects and events.

> "Art is long, and time is fleeting,
> And our hearts, though stout and brave,
> Still like muffled drums are beating
> Funeral marches to the grave."   LONGFELLOW.

SEVENTY-EIGHTH STUDY.

PLACES ON THE EARTH AND IN THE HEAVENS.

THERE is a place for every thing that God has made; and every thing is in its place.

EAST, rising up; the place where the sun rises.

Does the sun rise in the *east* ?

WEST, fall, or wasting; the part of heaven where the sun sets.

Does the sun set in the *west* ?

NORTH, roaring wind; the place in heaven where the pole star is.

Is the pole star in the *north* ?

SOUTH, softing, or hot; the place in heaven opposite the north.

Is the *south* opposite the north ?

GROUND, bottom, as of a lake; the surface of the earth.

Do we walk on the *ground* ?

EARTH, dust; the place where we live.

Is the *earth* our abode ?

ACRE, open or ploughed field; a piece of earth measured.

Is *acre* the name of an open field ?

FIELD, felled; ground not built on.

Does grass grow in the *field* ?

SEVENTY-NINTH STUDY.

RELATIVE PLACES.

PLACES, like the things which are in them, are related to one another, and to ourselves. They are near, above, below or without where we are.

HERE, the place where we are.

Is your book *here* ?

THERE, a place beyond where we are.

Is your teacher *there* ?

WHERE, at what place.

Where is the sun ?

THITHER, the place to which a thing goes.

Are you going *thither* ?

WHITHER, at what place.

Whither are you going ?

WITHIN, inside of a place.

Is your mother *within* ?

WITHOUT, outside of a place.

Is the well *without* the house ?

HENCE, from this place.

Will you go *hence* ?

HIGH, lifted up; above in place.

Is the sky *high* ?

LOW, cast down; not high in place.

Is the sea *low* ?

INWARD, towards a place.

Is the ship sailing *inward* ?

FAR, away in place.

Are you going *far* from home ?

FARTHER, more distant in place.

Did you go *farther* ?

OVER, above in place.

Is the sun *over* our heads ?

BELOW, laid down by; under in place.

Is the sea *below* us ?

NEAR, close by in place.

Do you like to be *near* home ?

BENEATH, low by; under in place.

Is the ground *beneath* us ?

NIGH, near in place.

Is the sky *nigh* the earth ?

OUT, beyond in place.

Has the girl gone *out ?*

OUTWARD, a going beyond in place.

    Is the ship bound *outward?*

BEYOND, at the outside in place.

    Is the sky *beyond* the earth ?

UP, high, or upon in place.

    Is the sun *up ?*

TOGETHER, in company ; brought near in place.

    Do the men work *together ?*

NEXT, nigh ; nearest in place.

    Is Monday *next* to Sunday ?

MIDDLE, coming between in place.

    Is the chair in the *middle* of the room ?

MID, inclosure ; between extreme points.

    Is it *mid*-day at noon ?

YONDER, gone ; distant in place.

    Do you see the sky *yonder ?*

EIGHTIETH STUDY.

LARGER DIVISIONS OF TIME.

"FAITH's steady eye alone illumes the eye,
    For time is pointing to eternity!"   R. A. WARE.

TIME, what passes ; the place of events—succession.

    Is *time* valuable ?

DAY, dawn ; the time the sun gives us light.

    Do we work in the *day ?*

SUNDAY, the sun's dawn ; the day of the sun.

    Was the sun worshipped on *Sunday* by the Saxons ?

MONDAY, the moon's dawn ; the day of the moon.

    Was the moon worshipped on *Monday ?*

TUESDAY, Tuisco's dawn ; the day of the god, Tuisco.

    Was Tuisco worshipped on *Tuesday ?*

WEDNESDAY, Woden's dawn ; the day of the god, Woden.

    Was Woden worshipped on *Wednesday ?*

THURSDAY, Thor's dawn ; the day of Thor, the thunder god.

    Was Thor worshipped on *Thursday ?*

FRIDAY, Frigga's dawn ; the day of the goddess, Frigga.

    Was Frigga worshipped on *Friday ?*

SATURDAY, Saturn's dawn ; the day of the planet, Saturn.

    Was Saturn worshipped on *Saturday ?*

NIGHT, declining ; the time the moon gives us light.

    Do we sleep at *night ?*

WEEK, the space of seven days.

    Does the *week* begin on Sunday ?

MONTH, the moonth ; the measure of the moon's course round the earth.

    How many days in a *month ?*

YEAR, a circle ; the measure of the earth's course round the sun.

How many days in a *year*?

Spring, shooting; the sprouting time.

Do plants sprout in *spring*?

Summer, warm; the sun or shiny time.

Is it hot in *summer*?

Fall, failing; the time of decay.

Do leaves fall in the *fall*?

Winter, the windy time; the time of winds.

Is it windy in *winter*?

Eastern, place of rising; the place where the sun rises.

Does the sun rise in the *eastern* heavens?

Lent, lengthing; the space of forty days from Ash Wednesday to Easter.

Do the Roman Catholics keep *Lent*?

EIGHTY-FIRST STUDY.

SMALLER DIVISIONS OF TIME.

"Like the swell of some sweet tune,
Morning rises into noon." Longfellow.

Morn, scattering; the first part of the day.

Does the sun rise at *morn*?

Morning, the opening of the day.

Is the *morning* the time for work?

Evening, declining; the close of the day.

Is it cool at *evening*?

Eventide, time of decline; the time of evening.

Is *eventide* a quiet time?

Noon, up, or limit; the place of the sun at twelve o'clock.

Is it warm at *noon*?

Night, declining or resting; the time of darkness.

Is *night* the time of rest?

Twilight, doubtful light; the time after sunset or before sunrise.

Is *twilight* pleasant?

Morrow, morning; the day after to-day.

Will the sun rise on the *morrow*?

Dawn, opening as rays; the first part of the day.

Does the sun make the *dawn*?

EIGHTY-SECOND STUDY.

RELATED DIVISIONS OF TIME.

"Like the swell of some sweet tune,
Morning changes into noon,
May glides onward into June." Longfellow.

Now, the present time.
  Should you study *now*?
Before, by the front; time before now.
  Is morning *before* noon?
Always, all going; time without end.
  Is the sun *always* moving?
Ever, at any time.
  Is God *ever* present with us?
Soon, early; at a set time.
  Will you go home *soon*?
Late, drawn out, or long; behind the set time.
  Were you *late* for school?
Early, shooting up; before the set time.
  May you go home *early*?
Again, turning, or front; once more.
  Say it *again*.

When, at what time.
  When will you come?
Then, at that time.
  May I *then* go?
While, staying; during a set time.
  Should you study *while* in school?
Yet, holding; still remaining.
  Are you going home *yet*?
Still, set, or firm; time up to the present.
  Are you *still* studying your lessons?
New, moving; fresh, or recent in time.
  Do you like *new* things?
Old, putting off; long made, or in use.
  Are some *old* things good?

EIGHTY THIRD STUDY.

RELATIONS OF THINGS AND EVENTS IN PLACE AND TIME.

ALL things have their places. All events have their times. We may compare these places and times, and mark their relations.

In, a cave; within, or inside.
  Are the chairs *in* the house?
Out, going forth; without, or outside.
  Has the child gone *out*?
To, end; to a certain place or time.
  Where do you go *to* school?
Of, out of, beginning; out of a certain place or time.
  Has the child gone out *of* the room?

From, source; beginning in a certain place or time.
  Does cotton come *from* the south?
Towards, looking at; fronting a certain place or time.
  Did the child go *towards* home?
By, being; being near in place and time.
  Is the child *by* the table?

WITH, joining; joined in place and time.

Is the child *with* the nurse?

NEAR, next; close by in place or time.

Should you stand *near* the fire?

ABOUT, bounds; round a place or time.

Is the dog *about* the house?

AROUND, a circle; going round a place or time.

Has the child gone *around* the house?

ABOVE, over; lifted up in place and time.

Are the clouds *above* the earth?

UNDER, on lower side; down in place or time.

Are fish *under* the water?

DOWN, dipping; low in place or time.

Has the moon gone *down*?

UP, high; aloft in place or time.

Is the sun *up*?

FOR, bearing; in place of.

Should you do good *for* evil?

THROUGH, passage; from side to side.

Did you go *through* the hall?

EIGHTY-FOURTH STUDY.

CONNECTION OF THINGS AND EVENTS IN PLACE AND TIME.

THINGS and events are connected. This we must notice carefully.

AND, giving; addition.

Have you a slate *and* pencil?

BUT, add; more or further.

Are our wants many, *but* light?

IF, granting; allowing or giving.

Will a child lie, *if* he is good?

THOUGH, allowing; granting it so.

Should we trust God, *though* He should slay us?

OR, one more; one in choice.

Can you write, *or* read?

AS, which, or it; like, or even.

Do you sit *as* you were told?

SO, that; in like manner.

Why are you *so* long in coming?

THAT, getting; in order to.

Do you study *that* you may be wise?

LEST, left; that not.

Should we be holy *lest* we die?

STILL, placing; to this time.

Are you *still* at work?

TILL, the while; to a certain time.

Will you wait *till* I come?

SINCE, seen; after a certain time.

Have you been well *since* I saw you?

THEN, placed; at that time.

Were you *then* happy?

ELSE, leaving off; otherwise.

Were you no where *else*?

YET, getting; still.

Are you *yet* idle?

THAN, set, or placed; compared with.

Is wisdom better *than* riches?

CHAPTER X.

GOD.

ALL things, when seen aright, make known to us something about God.   To know Him is life.

> "Let the first flower, corn-waving field, plain, tree,
> Here round my home, still lift my soul to THEE;
> And let me ever, midst thy bounties, raise
> An humble note of thankfulness and praise."   BLOOMFIELD.

EIGHTY-FIFTH STUDY.

GOD.

"GOD so loved the world as to give his only-begotten Son, that whosoever believeth in him should not perish, but have everlasting life."
                                                                    BIBLE.

GOD, strong and good; the Maker, Ruler and Redeemer of man.
    Is *God* love!
FATHER, the feeder; the Author of all things.
    Is God the *Father* of man!
SON, issue, or offspring; the second person in the Godhead.
    Did the *Son* die for man!

GHOST, breath or life; the soul, or mind.
    Is *ghost* the same as spirit !
HOLY, sound; free from all sin.
    Is God *holy!*
HOLY GHOST, the third person in the Godhead.
    Does the *Holy Ghost* teach man !

EIGHTY-SIXTH STUDY.

ATTRIBUTES OF GOD.

"THERE is none good, but one, and that is God."   BIBLE.

MIGHT, strong; strength or power.
    Is the *might* of God great!
ALMIGHTY, strong above all; having all power.
    Is God *almighty?*

KNOWLEDGE, what is held; understanding of things.
    Is *knowledge* useful !
WISDOM, power of holding; the right use of knowledge.

Is *wisdom* better than knowledge?

GOODNESS, state of being strong; kindness to all.
Is *goodness* due to all?

TRUTH, trust; what agrees with facts.
Should we always tell the *truth?*
HOLINESS, state of being sound; state of being free from sin.
Is *holiness* lovely?

EIGHTY-SEVENTH STUDY.

RELATION OF GOD TO MAN.

THE dearest name by which we can call God, is Father.

"Our Father, who art in heaven, hallowed be thy name."   BIBLE.

MAKER, one who does; the Creator of all things.
Is God the *Maker* of all?
RULER, one who guides; one who governs.
Is God the *Ruler* of the earth?
DAYSMAN, the dawn-man; one who makes peace.
Is Christ the *daysman?*
SHEPHERD, the sheep-watch; one who guides and tends sheep.
Is Christ the *Shepherd* of his people?
FATHER, the feeder; the Author of man.
Is God our *Father* as Creator?

PRIEST, one who stand before; one who waits at the altar.
Did the *priest* offer sacrifices?
HIGH, lifted up; distance upwards.
Are the heavens *high?*
HIGH-PRIEST, the priest who entered the holy of holies.
Was the *high-priest* above all others?
PEACE, settled down; a state of quiet.
Is *peace* a happy thing?
PEACE-MAKER, one who stops anger and makes quiet.
Is Christ the *peace-maker* between God and sinners?

EIGHTY-EIGHTH STUDY.

THE ABODE OF GOD.

"HEAVEN is my throne, and the earth is my footstool."   BIBLE.

EARTH, dust; the world in which we live.
Is the *earth* round?

HEAVEN, raised up, or arched; the region round the earth.
Does God fill *heaven* and earth?

CHAPTER XI.

QUALITIES OF THINGS.

No one is able to stop when he has named *things*. He wishes to do something more. He wishes to name his own *feelings*. The wood blazes in the stove. It is named fire. But fire acts upon us. We feel it. It is *warm*. We see it. It is *red* or *yellow*. It is *bright* also, and *sparkling*. These are some of its qualities.

We will now go back to home, and see some of its qualities. From home, we will go to the *house, household, callings* of men, and so on, over all the things we have named, gathering up their qualities and naming them. This is the way the mind grows. It first gets the *names* of THINGS; second, the *names* of QUALITIES.

EIGHTY-NINTH STUDY.

QUALITIES OF HOME.

"HOME, home! sweet, sweet home!
Be it ever so humble, there's no place like home."

SWEET, soothing; pleasing to the taste.

Is home *sweet*?

DEAR, rare; of great value.

Is home a *dear* place?

SMALL, thin; little in any way.

May a *small* house be neat?

OLD, falling off; a long time made.

Is an *old* house pleasant?

NEW, moving; lately made.

Does the child like his *new* house?

BARE, open; laid open to view.

Is the house *bare* of shingles?

HIGH, lifted up; raised far above us.

Is the chimney *high* above our heads?

Low, laid down; raised a little above the earth.

Is a hut a *low* house?

DARLING, little dear; much beloved.

Whose *darling* child are you?

NINETIETH STUDY.

QUALITIES OF OUTHOUSES.

THE old barn and snug wood-house peered through a small locust grove, and a white dove-cot stood by the garden gate.

LONG, drawn out; having length.
   Is the manger *long?*
NARROW, close; of little width.
   Is the stable *narrow?*
WIDE, spread; the space between the sides.
   Is the stall too *wide?*
CLEAN, open from; free from dirt.

Should the barn be *clean?*
OPEN, lifted off or up; not closed.
   Is a manger an *open* frame?
DRY, rubbed; free from moisture.
   Should all outhouses be *dry?*
WET, moist to the touch; containing moisture.
   Should a manger never be *wet?*

NINETY-FIRST STUDY.

QUALITIES OF HOUSEHOLD-STUFF.

"Now stir the fire and close the shutter fast,
   Let fall the curtains, wheel the sofa round;
   And while the bubbling and loud hissing urn
   Sends up a steamy column, and the cups
   That cheer, but not inebriate, wait on each,
   So let us welcome peaceful evening in."   COWPER.

NICE, tender; delicate or fine.
   Are chairs *nice?*
ROUGH, rugged; not polished, or even.
   Is the stove *rough?*
SMOOTH, soft; having an even surface.
   Is the table *smooth?*
HEAVY, heaved; having weight.

Is the inkstand *heavy?*
EVEN, smoothed down; level or smooth.
   Has the desk an *even* surface?
LIGHT, rising up; having little weight.
   Is a feather *light?*
SAME, like; like in some way.
   Is this the *same* old chair?

NINETY-SECOND STUDY.

QUALITIES OF THE HOUSEHOLD.

"SISTERS and brothers, little maid,
How many may you be !
How many ! seven in all, she said,
And wondering looked at me.",   WORDSWORTH.

GOOD, strong; kind. and comely.
Is a *good* father beloved !

BETTER, more advanced; more kind than another.
Is life *better* than raiment !

BEST, most advanced; more kind than all.
Is Jane the *best* sister of all !

KIND, knowing; tender in feelings.
Is a mother *kind* !

FAIR, clear to see; pleasant to behold.

Is a happy family *fair* to behold !

BUSY, closely attending; engaged in some pursuit.
Should we be always *busy* !

IDLE, ceasing; not actively employed.
Is an *idle* family poor !

GLAD, lifted up; pleased and joyous.
Are good children always *glad* !

GLEE, music; mirth or gayety.
Is the good child full of *glee* !

NINETY-THIRD STUDY.

QUALITIES OF FOOD.

"Is not the life more than meat, and the body than raiment !"—BIBLE.

FRESH, lively; new, lately made.
Do you like *fresh* bread !

ENOUGH, quieted; that which satisfies.
Has he eaten *enough* !

TART, sharp; sharp to the taste.
Are some apples very *tart* !

SOUR, what turns; sharp and biting to the taste.
Is a lemon *sour* !

NINETY-FOURTH STUDY.

QUALITIES OF CLOTHING.

"If pall and vair no more I wear,
Nor thou the crimson sheen,

As warm, we'll say, is the russet gray,
As gay the forest green."   SCOTT.

WARM, glowing; that which keeps heat.
    Does the child like a *warm* coat?
SOFT, mild to the touch; gentle and pleasant to the touch.
    Are silk gloves *soft?*
COOL, airy; not keeping heat.
    Are thread gloves *cool?*
THICK, pressed; of some distance from side to side.
    Are woollen clothes *thick?*
THIN, stretched; not thick.

Is lawn a *thin* kind of linen?
SILK, drawn fine; thread made by the silk-worm.
    Has the child a *silk* dress?
CHEAP, bargain; of low price and value.
    Is muslin a *cheap* cloth?
TIDY, beautiful; neat in dress.
    May a plain dress be *tidy?*
SHABBY, bare or shaven; worn and old.
    Are *shabby* garments pleasing?

NINETY-FIFTH STUDY.

QUALITIES OF MAN.

"IN every breast there burns an active flame,
The love of glory, or the dread of shame."   POPE.

WEAK, failing; feeble in strength.
    Is man a *weak* being?
EMPTY, void or idle; containing nothing.
    Has the man an *empty* head?
EARNEST, striving; ardor in business.
    Do you like an *earnest* person?

FICKLE, wavering; changeable.
    Do you despise a *fickle* person?
EVIL, pained; wicked or sinful.
    Have all men *evil* hearts?
DOUGHTY, able; brave or noble.
    Is a *doughty* man called a champion?

NINETY-SIXTH STUDY.

QUALITIES OF THE BODY OF MAN.

"OF stature tall and slender frame,
But firmly knit, was Malcolm Graeme."   SCOTT.

SOUND, whole; free from disease.

Is a *sound* body desirable !

STRONG, strained; having much power.

Must a *strong* man be healthy !

LITTLE, left or lessened; small in size.

May a *little* person be brave !

SICK, sighing; suffering from disease.

May a *sick* person be fretful !

HALE, whole; robust or sound.

Do you like to see a *hale* old man !

SPARE, pressed down; lean, wanting in flesh.

May a *spare* person be strong !

NINETY-SEVENTH STUDY.

QUALITIES OF PARTS OF THE BODY OF MAN.

"AND hazel was his eagle eye,
An auburn of the deepest dye
His short curled beard and hair."   SCOTT.

RUDDY, red; a healthy flesh color.

Is the face *ruddy* ?

NAKED, open; bare or uncovered.

Is the hand *naked* ?

WAN, passing away; pale in appearance.

Has the child a *wan* look !

WANE, failing or pale; pale or wanting color.

Have sick persons a *wan* look !

STERN, straining; severe and rigid.

Has the man a *stern* look !

UGLY, frank; wanting in what pleases.

Do you like an *ugly* face !

HOLLOW, a hole; sunken or depressed.

Has the sick person *hollow* cheeks !

HAGGARD, hacked or torn; worn and rough in looks.

Are the poor *haggard* ?

BROAD, spread out; extended in width.

Have Indians *broad* faces !

GRIM, fierce; having fierce looks

Do you like a *grim* face !

LANK, slack; yielding to the touch.

Are *lank* cheeks pleasing !

GAUNT, lean or wanting; thin and hollow.

Is an old horse *gaunt* ?

LEAN, thin; wanting in flesh.

Do you like a *lean* face !

FAT, plump, or fleshy.

Are infants *fat* ?

NINETY-EIGHTH STUDY.

QUALITIES OF THE SOUL.

" HE most lives,
Who thinks most, feels the noblest, acts the best."   BAILEY.

FREE, separated; having power to choose.

Is the soul *free*?

MAD, passionate; crazed or disordered in mind.

Does sorrow ever make the soul *mad*?

DARK, gloomy; obscured and gloomy.

Is a *dark* soul an evil one?

MEAN, common; base, of little value.

Is a *mean* soul happy?

STUBBORN, fixed; stiff-minded or obstinate.

Can a *stubborn* child be happy?

WICKED, turning away; evil in heart and life.

Are all men *wicked*?

RIGHT, straight; according to law.

Should we always do what is *right*?

SILLY, poor; weak in mind, foolish

Are some people *silly*?

NINETY-NINTH STUDY.

QUALITIES OF THE HUNTER AND HUNTING.

"REST thee, old hunter! the evening cool
  Will sweetly breathe on thy heated brow;
Thy dogs will lap of the shady pool,
  Thou art very weary—O rest thee now." P. BENJAMIN.

WILD, roving; roving or savage.

Does the hunter live a *wild* life?

READY, a going; quick and prepared.

Is a *ready* hunter a good hunter?

BOLD, forward; daring in action.

Should a hunter be *bold*?

QUICK, lively; swift and nimble

Who is *quick*?

ONE HUNDREDTH STUDY.

QUALITIES OF THE FISHER AND FISHING.

"Now, happy fisherman, now twitch the line!
  How the rod bends! behold the prize is thine!" GAY.

HARD, pressed; firm or strong.

Is a fisher's life *hard*?

LUSTY, extended; abounding in active power.

Is a *lusty* arm needed by the fisher?

STEADY, settled; firm and constant in mind.

Will a *steady* fisher succeed well?

STARK, stiff; strong, also gross.

Do you like a *stark* speech?

5*

ONE HUNDRED AND FIRST STUDY.

QUALITIES OF THE FARMER AND FARMING.

"How blest the farmer's simple life !
How pure the joy it yields !
Far from the world's tempestuous strife,
Free, 'mid the scented fields !"　　　　EVEREST.

BLITHE, gay and light; gay and joy-
ous.
　　Is the farmer *blithe ?*
TIRED, wasted; weary.
　　Should the *tired* farmer rest ?
FALLOW, failing; not tilled.
　　Is *fallow* land good ?
EARLY, shooting out; first in time.
　　Does the farmer rise *early ?*
LATE, drawn out so as to be long;
after the time.
　　Should the farmer be *late* at his
work ?

SULTRY, failing from heat; hot and
close.
　　Is *sultry* weather pleasant ?
COLD, blowing; wanting in heat.
　　Is *cold* weather healthy ?
DRY, rubbed; without moisture.
　　Does the farmer dread *dry* wea-
ther ?
STONY, firm or steady; full of stones.
　　Will the farmer clear the *stony*
ground ?
WET, moist; holding moisture.
　　Is *wet* land good ?

ONE HUNDRED AND SECOND STUDY.

QUALITIES OF WAR.

"THE horn and the trumpet are ringing afar,
As the summons to battle are sounding;
And the steed as he catches the signal of war,
In the pride of his spirit is bounding."　　　　PERCIVAL.

BLOOD, gushing; the vital fluid; also
slaughter.
　　Is *blood* the seat of bodily life ?
DEAD, sunk; having the properties
of death.

Is war a great evil ?
DREAD, shrunk; terror, or awe.
FOUL, pressed; filthy, or wicked.
　　Are *foul* deeds done in war ?

ONE HUNDRED AND THIRD STUDY.

QUALITIES OF MECHANICS AND THEIR CALLINGS.

"HE that hath a trade hath an estate; and he that hath a calling, hath an office of profit and honor."   FRANKLIN.

CRAFTY, skill or strength; full of art, or skill.

Can a good mechanic be *crafty?*

WISE, reaching, or holding; having much knowledge.

Should a mechanic be *wise?*

CUNNING, able or knowing; skilled in art.

Are some men *cunning* workmen?

ONE HUNDRED AND FOURTH STUDY.

QUALITIES OF THE MANUFACTURER AND MANUFACTURING.

"SILKS and satins, scarlets and velvets, put out the kitchen fire," as Poor Richard says.

MANY, crowd; numerous.

Are there *many* manufacturers?

SOME, taken together; a certain quantity.

Are *some* manufactures useful?

RAW, rough; not altered by man.

Is *raw* silk made into ribbons?

ALL, the whole; the whole number.

Are *all* manufactures used by men?

ONE HUNDRED AND FIFTH STUDY.

QUALITIES OF THE TRADER AND TRADING.

"IT is not more than twenty or thirty years since a young man going from any part of Scotland to England, of purpose to *carry the pack*, was considered, as going to lead the life, and acquire the fortune, of a gentleman."   HERON.

CHEAP, a bargain; having a low price.

Are *cheap* goods often bought?

FRESH, lively; lately made.

OLD, falling off; of long duration.

Do some traders sell *old* goods?

ONE HUNDRED AND SIXTH STUDY.

QUALITIES OF A SAILOR AND SAILOR'S LIFE.

"How cheery are the mariners,
    Those lovers of the sea!
Their hearts are like its yesty waves,
    As bounding and as free."   PARK BENJAMIN.

MERRY, brisk; gay and noisy.   Are sailors *merry?*

ONE HUNDRED AND SEVENTH STUDY.

QUALITIES OF THE LEARNED PROFESSIONS.

"STRIVE not too much for favor; seem at ease,
And rather pleased thyself, than bent to please."

CRABBE.

HIGH, lifted up; raised above us.   Are some wise men *wordy?*
    Is the gospel ministry a *high*   BLANK, white, or void; void or empty.
calling?   Is *blank* paper needed?
WORDY, full of words.

ONE HUNDRED AND EIGHTH STUDY.

QUALITIES OF OFFICERS AND OFFICES.

"THE man whom Heaven appoints
    To govern others, should himself first learn
    To bend his passions to the sway of reason."

THOMSON.

FIRST, most advanced; before all   Has a *prime* minister a high
    others.   office?
    Does the President fill the *first*   MILD, smooth; kind and gentle.
office?   Should a ruler be *mild?*
PRIME, beginning or first; highest in   STERN, set or stiff; severe and stiff.
    rank.   Are *stern* officers beloved?

ONE HUNDRED AND NINTH STUDY.

QUALITIES OF THE WORKS OF MAN.

"MAN has sought out many inventions."   BIBLE.

LIKE, even; nearly the same.
  Are the works of man *like* God!
LITTLE, less; small in size.
KEEN, piercing; sharp in cutting.
  Is a new knife *keen?*

SHARP, cutting; having a thin edge
  or point.
  Has a needle a *sharp* point?
LEVEL, pressed down smooth; flat,
  not rough.
  Is the table *level?*

ONE HUNDRED AND TENTH STUDY

QUALITIES OF THE WORKS OF GOD.

"THE gentle moon, the kindling sun,
  The many stars are given,
As shrines to burn earth's incense on,
  The altar-fires of heaven."   WHITTIER.

GREAT, increasing; large in size or
  number.
  Are the works of God *great?*
GOOD, strong; of fine quality.
  Is God a *good* being!

HOT, rousing; having much heat.
  Are the rays of the sun *hot?*
BLEAK, open; open to the wind.
  The hills are *bleak.*

ONE HUNDRED AND ELEVENTH STUDY.

QUALITIES OF MINERAL BODIES.

"ALONE I walked the ocean strand;
  A pearly shell was in my hand:
I stoop'd and wrote upon the sand
  My name, the year, the day."   HANNAH GOULD.

HARD, pressed; firm to the touch.
  Are all metals *hard?*
ACID, sharp edge; sharp to the taste.
  Is aluminum an *acid* metal?

BRIGHT, darting, as rays; shiny.
  Is gold a *bright* metal?
BRITTLE, breaking; easily broken.
  Is chalk *brittle?*

ONE HUNDRED AND TWELFTH STUDY.

QUALITIES OF VEGETABLE BODIES.

> "HEAP'D in the hollows of the grove,
>   The wither'd leaves lie dead;
> They rustle to the eddying gust,
>   And to the rabbit's tread."   BRYANT.

RANK, reaching; strong in growth.
  Are some plants *rank?*

SHORT, cut off; low or of small height.
  Is grass *short?*

PRETTY, set off; neat and pleasing.
  Are all flowers *pretty?*

TOUGH, pulling; that which may be bent.
  Is hickory wood *tough?*

MELLOW, soft, or melting; soft with ripeness.
  Are peaches *mellow?*

RIPE, what may be reaped; mature in growth.
  Are *ripe* pears pleasant to the taste?

WHOLE, sound; all, every part, or one.
  Is the plant *whole?*

ONE HUNDRED AND THIRTEENTH STUDY.

QUALITIES OF ANIMALS.

> "HARK! is that the angry howl
>   Of the wolf, the hills among?——
> Or the hooting of the owl,
>   On his leafy cradle swung?"   WHITTIER.

STRAY, scattered; wandering, or lost.
  Have you seen a *stray* lamb?

TAME, subdue; accustomed to man.
  Is the ox *tame?*

GREEDY, reaching forward; having a strong desire for food.
  Are vultures *greedy* animals?

RAMPANT, rearing up, or overleaping.
  What is a lion *rampant?*

SWIFT, whirling; rapid in motion.
  Is the deer *swift* in running.

SLOW, slack; lazy in motion.
  Are snails *slow* animals?

ONE HUNDRED AND FOURTEENTH STUDY.

QUALITIES OF LIGHT.

> "My heart looks up when I behold
> A rainbow in the sky." WORDSWORTH.

RED, opening or glowing; a bright warm color.
Are some apples *red?*
YELLOW, bright; a bright color.
Is gold a *yellow* metal?
GREEN, growing as a grass; a cool color composed of yellow and blue.
Is moss *green?*
BLUE, a rich warm color.

Is the sky *blue?*
BROWN, burnt; a sober cool color.
Are some kind of woods *brown?*
GRAY, fair; white mixed with black.
Is an old man's hair *gray?*
BLACK, waning, or pale; the color of night.
Are clouds sometimes *black?*

ONE HUNDRED AND FIFTEENTH STUDY.

QUALITIES OF GOD.

> "God of wisdom, God of might,
> Father! dearest name of all,
> Bow thy throne and bless our rite;
> 'Tis thy children on thee call." SPRAGUE.

BLESSED, made blithe; made happy.
Is a Christian blessed?
MIGHTY, strength; strong.
Is God *mighty?*
FIRST, advanced before; the beginning of all things.

Is God our *first* ruler?
TRUE, closed fast; real, or according to fact.
Is there but one *true* God?
HOLY, whole, or sound; free from sin.
Is God *holy* in all his ways?

CHAPTER XII.

ACTIONS.

WE have now come to the THIRD stage of the mind in gathering up words—ACTIONS. We began with the *names of things;* as *papa, mamma, dog.* We then got the *names of some qualities;* as *good* papa, *dear* mamma, *bad* dog. Afterwards, we got the *names of actions;* as, good papa *comes,* dear mamma *sings,* bad dog *bites.* In this way, every child gathers up the words that form his daily speech.

Our old Saxon forefathers formed nearly all names of ACTIONS from names of *things.* They did so by putting *gan,* to go, *anan,* to give, or *agan,* to hold, after the names of things. Thus *deal,* the name of a part, becomes *dealan,* to divide into parts.

ONE HUNDRED AND SIXTEENTH STUDY.

ACTIONS OF THE BODY OF MEN.

THE body has its own actions. The pulse beats and the lungs breathe even while we sleep. But our bodies cease to act.

> "THEY walked not under the lindens,
> They played not in the hall;
> But shadow, and silence, and sadness
> Were hanging over all."   LONGFELLOW.

SIT, to cast down; to rest on a seat.
Can you *sit* on a chair?

LIE, to throw down; to rest stretched out.
Do you *lie* in bed?

SLUMBER, to murmur in breathing; to take light sleep.
May he *slumber* in school?

SLEEP, to be loose; to rest unknowingly.
Do we *sleep* at night?

SNORE, to make a sound with the nose; to breathe with a hoarse voice in sleep.
Can you *snore* loudly?

RISE, to lift up oneself; to get up from sleep, or sitting.
Do you *rise* in the morning?

SNEEZE, to thrust out air; to emit air audibly through the nose.
Do you *sneeze* when you have a cold?

PAIN, to prickle; to produce an uneasy feeling.
Does severe cold *pain* us?

NAP, to nod; to take a short sleep.
Does grandfather *nap* in his chair?

SPIT, to cast out; to cast out from the mouth.

Should we *spit* on the carpet?
Swoon, to fall away; to sink into a fainting state.

Have you ever seen any one *swoon?*

ONE HUNDRED AND SEVENTEENTH STUDY.

ACTIONS OF THE HANDS.

> "She stood beside the well her God had given,
> To gush in that deep wilderness, and bathed
> The forehead of her child, until he laughed
> In his reviving happiness, and lisped
> His infant thoughts of gladness at the sight
> Of the cool plashing of his mother's hand."
>
> N. P. Willis.

Hand, to thrust out; to reach any thing with the hand.
Did you *hand* the book?
Handle, to hold; to feel or use with the hand.
Can you *handle* the hoe?
Hold, to strain; to keep fast.
Can you *hold* a horse?
Creep, to grapple; to crawl on the hands and feet.
Do infants *creep?*
Grope, to feel; to feel with the hands.
Do we *grope* with the hands?
Gripe, to catch; to seize with the hand.
Did you *gripe* the toy?
Grapple, to seize; to lay fast hold of.
Did the boys *grapple?*
Clutch, to close fast; to clasp with the hand.
Did the boy *clutch* the knife?

Clap, to strike; to strike the hands together.
Did you *clap* the speaker?
Clip, to drive quickly; to cut with shears.
Do we *clip* the box in summer?
Strike, to rub or thrust; to hit with any thing, as the hands.
Should children *strike* each other?
Stroke, to rub gently; to rub gently and soothe.
Do we *stroke* the kitten?
Box, to close up; to strike with the fist.
Do good boys *box?*
Finger, to thrust out; to catch with the fingers.
Do you *finger* your book?
Reach, to stretch; to put out the hand.
Can you *reach* across the table?

ONE HUNDRED AND EIGHTEENTH STUDY.

ACTIONS OF THE FEET.

> " For thou didst tread
> The way that leads me heavenward, and
> My often wayward footsteps led
> In the same path with patient hand."

> G. W. BETHUNE.

WALK, to roll, or press; to move on the feet.

　Do you like to *walk?*

SNEAK, to creep softly; to move in a crouching way.

　Do the wicked *sneak* away?

LEAP, to draw up; to bound or spring forward.

　Can you *leap* far?

RUN, to rush; to move quickly on the feet.

　Do children like to *run?*

STAND, to place; to be upon the feet.

　Should you *stand* straight?

STALK, to steal along; to walk with a high proud step.

SLIP, to move easily; to slide on the feet.

　Did you *slip?*

SLIDE, to move smoothly; to move along without stepping.

　Can you *slide* on the ice?

STRIDE, to step, or open; to walk with long steps.

　Does the farmer *stride* over the field?

WADE, to go through; to walk through water.

　Do you like to *wade* in water?

WADDLE, to go; to move from side to side in walking.

　Should we *waddle* when we walk?

STEP, to open out; to move the foot.

　Do we *step* in walking?

FETTER, to tie the feet; to bind with a chain.

　Does the jailer *fetter* the criminal?

ONE HUNDRED AND NINETEENTH STUDY.

ACTIONS OF MAN.

MAN is active, both when he sleeps and when he awakes. He dreams of happiness.

> " Do something—do it soon—with all thy might;
> An angel's wing would droop if long at rest,
> And God himself inactive were no longer blest."

> CARLOS WILCOX.

LIVE, to breathe on; to have life.
Does man *live?*

GROW, to swell; to increase in size.
May the boy *grow?*

HAVE, to seize; to possess.
Have you a book?

Do, to be able; to make or perform.
Will you *do* what is right?

LAUGH, to thrust; to make the noise of mirth.
Can you *laugh* loudly?

SIGH, to draw in; to draw in and exhale a deep breath.
Do those in pain *sigh?*

WEEP, to cry out; to shed tears.
Do you often *weep?*

LIFT, to raise into the air; to raise up from the ground.
Can you *lift* a chair?

BROOK, to grind the teeth; to bear or endure a check.
Can children *brook* restraint?

BEAR, to bring forth; to carry, or support.
Can you bear much *weight?*

AIL, to be in pain; to be sick, or troubled.
What *ails* you?

BELIEVE, to leave with; to trust on a person or thing.
Do all *believe* in God?

WORSHIP, to give honor; to adore God.
Do you love to *worship* God?

HALLOW, to make sound; to make holy.
Should we *hallow* the name of God?

ONE HUNDRED AND TWENTIETH STUDY.

ACTIONS IN THE HOUSEHOLD.

"AROUND his board his wife and children smile:
Communion sweetest, nature here can give,
Each find endearments, office of delight
With love and duty blending."   TIMOTHY DWIGHT.

GREET, to cry out; to speak and address one kindly.
Should we *greet* each other every morning?

KISS, to fall; to salute or greet with the lips.
Do you *kiss* your mother every night?

ASK, to press upon; to seek by speech.
Do you *ask* your parents to teach you?

ANSWER, to speak back; to speak when questioned.
Do you *answer* your parents kindly?

MEET, to fall to; to come together.
Do children *meet* their parents gladly in the morning?

PART, to break; to separate from each other.
Do we *part* at night?

BEGIN, to go in; to commence any thing.

Do you *begin* to study early !

BURY, to hide or cover; to put a body in the earth.

Do we *bury* the dead in sorrow !

SWEAR, to lay *to*; to bear witness by appealing to God.

Should men *swear !*

TAUNT, to tug; to accuse with cutting words.

Is it unkind to *taunt !*

GLIDE, to go gently; to move lightly along the surface.

Does the boy *glide* over the ice !

YAWN, to open; to have the mouth open through drowsiness.

Does the sleepy boy *yawn !*

GAPE, to tear open; to open the mouth wide.

Do we often *gape* after eating !

Bow, to bend as a bow; to bend the head.

Should we *bow* to those we know !

WRIGGLE, to move twistingly; to move with short twists.

Do some children *wriggle* when they walk !

ONE HUNDRED AND TWENTY-FIRST STUDY.

ACTIONS OF THE SENSES.

THE five senses, *hearing, seeing, smell, taste* and *touch*, are active, waiting upon the soul. They tell us many things about the world.

" UPON the sodden ground
His old right hand lay nerveless, listless, dead,
Unsceptered; and his realmless eyes were closed,
While his bowed head seemed listening to the earth." KEATS.

LOOK, to stretch forth; to turn the eye towards an object.

Does the eye *look* at things !

BLINK, to glitter; to twinkle with the eyes.

Do we *blink* in strong light !

STARE, to strain stiff; to look with fixed eye.

Should we *stare* at any one !

HARK, to direct the ear; to lend the ear.

Do you *hark* when you hear a noise !

HEARKEN, to lend the ear; to listen to what is said.

Should you *hearken* to your teacher !

LIST, to incline forward; to incline the ear in desire.

Do you *list* to what is said !

SMELL, to relax; to know by the nose.

Can you *smell* the flowers !

FEEL, to touch; to know by the touch.

Can you *feel* the round table.

LISTEN, to lend the ear; to give attention to what is said.

Must you *listen* if you would learn !

SEEK, to stretch out the eye; to search for any thing.

Should we *seek* wisdom !

ONE HUNDRED AND TWENTY-SECOND STUDY.

ACTIONS OF THE SOUL OF MAN.

THE soul, we have reason to believe, never sleeps. It is so active as to have no desire to rest.

> " MAN superior walks
> Amid the glad creation, musing praise,
> And looking lively gratitude."　　THOMSON.

SPEAK, to thrust out; to tell our thoughts by words.

Do we *speak* often ?

STUN, to strike by noise; to make senseless.

Did the fall *stun* him ?

WONDER, to turn; to look or be surprised.

Does the mind *wonder*

THINK, to set in the mind; to exercise the mind about any thing.

Do we *think* always?

KNOW, to hold in the mind; to be acquainted with any thing.

Do you *know* any thing about the sun ?

GLAD, to be lifted up; to cheer with pleasure.

Does God *glad* the heart of man?

MOURN, to murmur to oneself; to sorrow for that which is lost.

Does the mother mourn for her child ?

WISH, to long for; to long for something.

Do you *wish* to be good?

LIKE, to stroke smoothly; to be pleased with.

Can you *like* a bad child?

CHIDE, to press with words; to blame lightly.

Does your teacher *chide* you when you do wrong?

LIGHT, to shoot out; to make things visible.

Does knowledge *light* up the mind?

CRAZE, to crack; to make one mad.

Does sorrow *craze* the brain?

RECKON, to stretch so as to tell; to count or number.

Can you *reckon* as far as ten?

HEED, to give attention; to mind with care.

Do you *heed* what your mother says?

PROVE, to try, as by taste; to try so as to find the truth.

Should we be able to *prove* whatever we do?

HOPE, to reach forward; to desire future good.

Do you *hope* to go to heaven?

WEEP, to cry out; to shed tears.

Do we *weep* for the dead?

LOVE, to lean forward; to delight in any thing.

Do you *love* God?

MOAN, to make a low sound; to express sorrow.

    Do we *moan* in grief?

HATE, to be hot; to dislike greatly.

    Do you *hate* wickedness?

LOATHE, to thrust away; to feel much disgust.

    Do the sick *loathe* food?

WILL, to set forward; to choose any thing.

    Do you *will* before you walk?

RECK, to tell; to care or mind.

    Do the dead *reck* any thing?

ONE HUNDRED AND TWENTY-THIRD STUDY.

ACTIONS AND FOOD.

"RETIRED
Within his gorgeous hall, Assyria's king
Sits at the banquet, and in love and wine
Revels delighted."   ATHERSTONE.

COOK, to prepare food for eating.

    Is it easy to *cook* food?

SIFT, to separate; to take the coarse from the fine with a sieve.

    Do we *sift* meal?

KNEAD, to press with the fist; to make flour and barm into dough.

    Does the girl *knead* the dough?

BAKE, to harden by fire; to cook food in an oven.

    Do we *bake* bread in an oven?

DINE, to take the day meal; to eat the chief meal.

    Do you *dine* at two o'clock?

CARVE, to pluck; to cut in small pieces.

    Is it easy to *carve* a fowl?

CRAM, to force into; to stuff in any thing as food.

    Does the child *cram* food into his mouth?

CHOKE, to stop up; to stop the windpipe.

    Will a bone *choke* you?

SUP, to make a noise with the lips in taking large quantities; to take up with the mouth.

    Do you *sup* fast?

SIP, to make a noise with the lips in taking small quantities; to take up with the lips.

    Do we *sip* our tea?

DRINK, to draw; to swallow liquor or water.

    Do children *drink* much?

GRIND, to rub; to reduce to powder.

    Does the girl *grind* the coffee?

SMACK, noise in tasting; to make a noise with the lips.

    Is it nice to *smack*?

ONE HUNDRED AND TWENTY-FOURTH STUDY.

ACTIONS AND CLOTHING.

"THE old man sunk
Upon his knees, and in the drapery
Of the rich curtains buried up his face." N. P. WILLIS.

CLOTHE, to draw over; to put garments on the body.

Does the mother *clothe* her child?

DECK, to cover; to dress finely.

Does the mother *deck* her child?

DYE, to color; to tinge by coloring.

Can we *dye* garments?

KNIT, to make by knots; to make by knotting threads.

Does the girl *knit* gloves?

ONE HUNDRED AND TWENTY-FIFTH STUDY.

ACTIONS IN THE HOUSE.

"HER wheel at rest, the matron thrills no more
With treasured tales and legendary lore.
All, all are fled."   ROGERS.

SCREEN, to cut off; to shade from heat or cold.

Does the house *screen* you from cold?

SAY, to thrust out; to speak or tell any thing.

Can the baby *say* any thing?

SCORCH, to dry up; to burn on the surface.

Will the fire *scorch* clothes?

CLEAN, to remove; to separate from any thing dirty.

Does the housemaid *clean* the room?

SWEEP, to wipe; to clean by brushing.

Will the girl *sweep* the stairs?

WASH, to clean by rubbing in water.

Will the girl *wash* the dirty clothes?

WIPE, to rub dry; to rub for the purpose of cleaning.

Did the girl *wipe* the floor this morning?

SPILL, to waste; to let run out of a vessel.

Did you *spill* the milk?

WHITTLE, a knife; to pare with a knife.

Do boys *whittle* sticks.

SEND, to urge; to cause to go.

Can you *send* a book?

SMOTHER, to smoke; to choke in any way.

Would smoke *smother* you?

Smooth, to make even; to give an even surface to.

Do we *smooth* clothes

Bide, to lodge; to stay in a place, or dwell.

Do children *bide* at home?

Break, to thrust; to drive in pieces.

Will a fall *break* a plate?

Quench, to put out; to put out as a flame.

Will water *quench* fire?

Rest, to lay down; to cease from work.

Do we *rest* at night?

Rouse, to shake; to stir up to action.

Shall I *rouse* you in the morning?

ONE HUNDRED AND TWENTY-SIXTH STUDY.

ACTIONS OF THE HOUSEKEEPER.

"At intervals my mother's voice was heard
Urging despatch: briskly the work went on,
All hands employed to wash, to rinse, to wring,
To fold, to starch, and clap, and iron and plait."

BARBAULD.

Foster, to give food; to feed, or bring up.

Does the kind lady *foster* many children?

Warm, to rouse with heat; to supply heat.

Does the fire *warm* you?

Feed, to nourish; to give food.

Does the nurse *feed* the children?

Sew, to stitch; to unite with needle and thread.

Will you *sew* your glove?

Hem, to fold and sew down the edge.

Can you *hem* your handkerchief?

Swaddle, to clothe; to bind with bandage.

Will the nurse *swaddle* the child?

Tie, to strain; to bind with a cord or band.

Will you *tie* your shoe?

Singe, to crackle in scorching; to burn a little.

Will you *singe* your dress if you stand too near the fire?

Soak, to suck in: to steep in liquid.

Will the girl *soak* the muslin in water?

Rear, to erect; to raise or bring up.

Will the family *rear* the child?

Milk, to stroke gently; to obtain milk by stroking.

Does the girl *milk* the cow?

Rinse, to remove by washing; to cleanse by water.

Do we *rinse* clothes after they have been washed?

Wring, to strain; to strain and twist round.

Does the girl *wring* the clothes?

Churn, to turn or shake; to shake milk into butter.

Does the girl *churn* to-day?

ONE HUNDRED AND TWENTY-SEVENTH STUDY.

ACTIONS OF THE HOUSEHOLDER.

"STRIKE till the last armed foe expires;
Strike for your altars and your fires;
Strike for the green graves of your sires;
God—and your native land."　　　HALLECK.

OPEN, to lift off; to take away any fastening.

Does the householder *open* the house?

SHUT, to bolt; to close with fastenings.

Is the house *shut* up?

GIVE, to send to; to bestow any thing upon any one.

Is it pleasant to *give?*

WORK, to strive; to perform labor.

Does the man *work* well?

LEAD, to draw forward; to guide or conduct.

Should a father *lead* his children?

RULE, to direct; to order or control.

Should a father *rule* his children.

BID, to drive out the voice; to command or direct.

Should you do as your father *bids* you?

BIDE, to stay; to dwell or continue.

Will you *bide* long in this house?

BEQUEATH, to say by will; to leave any thing by will.

Did your mother *bequeath* you the money?

HUSBAND, to keep in the house; to use carefully.

Should the farmer *husband* his hay?

ONE HUNDRED AND TWENTY-EIGHTH STUDY.

ACTIONS OF THE HUNTER.

"BUT dauntless he, nor chart, nor journey's plan
In woods required, whose trained eye was keen
As eagle of the wilderness, to scan
His path, by mountain, swamp or deep ravine."
　　　CAMPBELL.

HUNT, to rush; to chase wild animals.

Do many men *hunt* wild animals?

TRAP, to catch up; to catch by a snare.

Did the hunter *trap* the beaver?

RUN, to rush; to pass rapidly on foot.

Can the hunter *run* after game?

RIDE, to go forward; to go on horseback.

Will the hunter *ride* far?

BET, to give a pledge; to stake a wager.

Is it wrong to *bet?*

WEARY, to wear down; to tire the body.

Does the chase *weary* the hunter?

SLAY, to strike; to put to death by violence.

Will the hunter *slay* the deer?

SKIN, to strip; to take off the skin.

Has the hunter *skinned* the animal?

THROW, to hurl; to fling or cast away.

Does the hunter *throw* his spear?

FORD, to pass; to cross a river by walking on the bottom.

Does the hunter *ford* many rivers?

FLAY, to bark; to strip off the skin.

May the hunter *flay* an animal?

GAD, to go; to wander about.

Does the hunter *gad* about?

SHUN, to go from; to keep out of sight.

ONE HUNDRED AND TWENTY-NINTH STUDY.

ACTIONS OF THE FISHER.

"A LITTLE hovel by the river side
Received us: there hard labor and the skill
In fishing, which was formerly my sport,
Supported life."   HOME.

FISH, to take fish; to try to take fish.

Is it pleasant to *fish?*

HOOK, to catch with a bent piece of metal.

Does the fisher *hook* fish?

SPEAR, to pierce; to kill or pierce with the spear.

Does the fisher *spear* eels?

DRAG, to haul along; to pull or haul.

Will the fisher *drag* in the net?

SAIL, to strain in a course; to pass through water in a vessel.

Has the fisher to *sail* much?

SWIM, to vanish; to pass through water by using the limbs.

Is it dangerous to *swim?*

WRECK, to break; to dash on rocks or shoals, as a ship.

Was the vessel *wrecked?*

SWAMP, to suck down; to upset in water.

Will the boat *swamp?*

PULL, to drag or haul.

Does the fisherman *pull* in the net full of fish?

WEATHER, to outride a storm; to bear up through a storm.

Will a strong ship *weather* a storm?

STEER, to strain towards; to direct, as a vessel.

Does the pilot *steer* the ship?

ROW, to urge; to drive with oars.

Do boatmen *row* the boat!

TOIL, to strain; to labor; to become weary.

Do laborers *toil* daily?

BAIT, to feed; to put meat on a hook or in a snare.

Do fishers *bait* their hooks?

'ONE HUNDRED AND THIRTIETH STUDY.

ACTIONS OF THE FARMER.

"THE farmer's life displays in every part
A moral lesson to the sensual heart.
Though in the lap of plenty, thoughtful still,
He looks beyond the present, good or ill."

BLOOMFIELD.

FARM, to produce corn; to cultivate or lease land.

Is it healthy to *farm?*

TILL, to put in order; to cultivate land.

Does the farmer *till* his land?

SEED, to scatter; to sow the land with seed.

Do farmers *seed* their lands?

WEED, to free from noxious plants.

Will the gardener *weed* the garden?

HARVEST, to be cold or keen; to gather in grain or fruits.

Does the farmer *harvest* the wheat?

STABLE, to put in a stall; to put in a stable or barn.

Should the farmer *stable* his cattle in winter?

STALL, to stand; to put in a stable or stand.

Do we *stall* cattle?

PEN, to close up; to put in a fold.

Does the farmer *pen* his sheep?

PLOUGH, to thrust; to turn up the soil with a plough.

Do we *plough* in spring?

REAP, to cut; to cut grain with a sickle.

Will the farmer *reap* in the fall?

DIG, to thrust; to turn up the ground with a spade.

Must the farmer *dig?*

SHOVEL, to shove; to throw up earth with a shovel.

Can you *shovel* sand?

HOE, to chop; to scrape or dig with a hoe.

Will the man *hoe* the garden beds?

RAKE, to scrape; to gather grass or grain with a rake.

Does he *rake* the hay together?

THRASH, to beat; to beat out grain from the husk.

Can he *thrash* with a flail?

MOW, to cut off; to cut grass with a scythe.

Can he *mow* with a scythe?

HINDER, to weaken; to keep back or obstruct.

Does rain *hinder* the farmer from working?

SUMMER, to pass the hot season; to pass or carry through summer.

Do we *summer* cattle?

WINTER, to pass the windy season; to pass or carry through winter.

Do cattle *winter* well on good fodder?

FAN, to open; to separate chaff from grain.

Will he *fan* wheat?

HIRE, to get wages; to engage for a reward or price.

Does the farmer *hire* many men?

GATHER, to close up or bind; to bring into stores, or heap up.

Will they *gather* in all the grain at harvest?

EARN, to gather; to obtain by labor.

Does the laborer *earn* much?

GATHER, to go through; to collect into one place.

Does the farmer *gather* his grain?

ONE HUNDRED AND THIRTY-FIRST STUDY.

ACTIONS OF THE HOUSEWRIGHT.

> "AT art's command,
> The village grows, the city springs."   SPRAGUE.

SUNDER, to part; to separate in any way.

Does the housewright *sunder* the wood?

FRAME, to join; to form the outline of a building.

Did the housewright *frame* the barn?

FLOOR, to make flat; to lay the bottom part of a house or room.

Will the carpenter *floor* the house?

ROOF, to cover; to put on the cover of a house.

When did the man *roof* the house?

BOARD, to spread; to cover with boards.

Do we *board* houses?

BUILD, to set or make; to frame and raise a building.

Will they *build* a large house?

SAW, to cut; to cut with a saw.

Can the man *saw* wood?

BORE, to thrust; to make holes with a gimlet.

Will the carpenter *bore* a hole in the wood?

ONE HUNDRED AND THIRTY-SECOND STUDY.

ACTIONS OF THE WHEELWRIGHT.

"GOD made the prophet's wheel,
And filled it full of eyes."

WHET, to sharpen; to make sharp by rubbing.

TURN, to move in a circle; to form on a lathe.

Does the wheelwright *turn* the hub?

HEW, to strike; to cut with any instrument.

Does he *hew* his spokes?

CLEAVE, to split; to divide by cutting.

Do we *cleave* wood with an axe?

ONE HUNDRED AND THIRTY-THIRD STUDY.

ACTIONS OF THE SHIPWRIGHT.

"HER keel hath struck on a hidden rock,
Her planks are torn asunder;
And down came her masts with a reeling shock."

WILSON.

TRIM, to make firm; to put in order.

SHAPE, to form; to give form to any thing.

Does the shipwright *shape* his vessel?

FASTEN, to hold firm; to make firm.

Does the shipwright *fasten* the beams?

WIELD, to strain forcibly; to sway with the hand.

Does he *wield* a large axe?

DECK, to throw on; to furnish with a deck.

Does he *deck* the vessel with boards?

RIB, to give sides; to enclose with ribs.

Does he *rib* the ship?

ONE HUNDRED AND THIRTY-FOURTH STUDY.

ACTIONS OF THE MILLWRIGHT.

"UPON the river's bank,
Near by the sounding waterfall,
He built the village mill."

DAM, to stop; to keep in water with a bank.

Does the millwright *dam* the water?

DRILL, to twist; to bore with a drill.

Does he *drill* holes in the plank?

ONE HUNDRED AND THIRTY-FIFTH STUDY.

ACTIONS OF THE SMITH.

"THE smith, a mighty man is he,
    With large and sinewy hands;
And the muscles of his brawny arms
    Are strong as iron bands." LONGFELLOW.

BEAT, to strike; to strike often.
    Does the smith *beat* the iron?
NAIL, to pin; to fasten with nails or iron pins.
    Is the horseshoe *nailed* on?
HEAT, to warm; to warm by fire.
    Will the smith *heat* the metal?

MELT, to soften; to make like a liquid.
    Can one *melt* silver?
HAMMER, to beat; to strike with a hammer.
    Is the iron well *hammered*?
NEAL, to kindle; to temper by heat.
    Does the mechanic *neal* iron?

ONE HUNDRED AND THIRTY-SIXTH STUDY.

ACTIONS OF THE WEAVER.

"IN olden time,
Kings' daughters had their looms."

WEAVE, to throng; to unite threads and form cloth.
    Will he *weave* fine cloth?
SPIN, to draw out; to draw out flax or wool into a thread.
    Do women *spin*?

TWIST, to turn about; to wind one thread round another.
    Does the weaver *twist* his cord?
KNOT, to swell; to join or unite threads or cords.
    Can the weaver *knot* his thread?

ONE HUNDRED AND THIRTY-SEVENTH STUDY.

ACTIONS OF THE MANUFACTURER.

"A THOUSAND rivers minister to man:
They irrigate the soil, and turn the wheels
Of busy workshops."

SHAPE, to form; to form for some end.
    Does the pin-maker *shape* his pins?

FULL, to tread; to thicken cloth in a mill.
    Do men *full* cloth?

BLEACH, to whiten; to make white by taking away the color.
    Do we *bleach* muslin?

COMB, to scrape; to separate and arrange with a comb.
    Do they *comb* flax at a mill?

GRIND, to make smooth or sharpen.
    Can you *grind* a knife to make it sharp?

GLAZE, to make blue; to cover over with shining matter.
    Are many dishes *glazed?*

BRAND, to burn; to mark in any way.
    Does the manufacturer *brand* his goods?

GAIN, to obtain; to get by labor or gift.
    Does the idle man *gain* much?

ONE HUNDRED AND THIRTY-EIGHTH STUDY.

ACTIONS OF THE TRADER.

"TRADE is the pulse of nations,
And on its healthful throbbings hang
The industry of millions."

HAVE, to hold; to hold or possess.
    Can the trader *have* many things?

WEND, to go or turn; to go from place to place.
    Does the trader *wend* his way alone?

DUN, to crave noisily; to ask often for payment.
    Will the merchant *dun* if he is not paid?

LIE, to stretch; to tell an untruth.
    Should a man *lie?*

CHEAPEN, to strike a bargain; to ask the price.
    Do some wish to *cheapen* all goods?

METE, to reach to; to measure.
    Does the miller *mete* out the corn?

SHIP, to put in shape; to put on a ship.

Will the merchant *ship* tea from China here?

WEIGH, to balance; to find the quantity of a thing by weighing it.

Does the grocer *weigh* tea?

DEAL, to divide; to trade in any thing.

Does he *deal* in wines?

BUY, to get things by paying for them.

Will he *buy* many things?

STORE, to hoard; to lay up goods.

Should the trader *store* his goods in winter?

SELL, to send to; to give away a thing for money.

Does the trader *sell* much?

BARGAIN, to lend; to make some contract, buy or sell.

Can you *bargain?*

ONE HUNDRED AND THIRTY-NINTH STUDY.

ACTIONS OF THE SOLDIER.

"AH, never shall the land forget
How gushed the life-blood of her brave—
Gushed, warm with hope and courage yet,
Upon the soil they sought to save."   BRYANT.

WREST, to twist; to gain by force.

Can the soldier *wrest* the goods of the enemy?

WARD, to keep off.

Does he *ward* the blows?

QUELL, to press down; to overcome.

Can the officer *quell* the fight?

RUSH, to move forcibly; to move with violence.

Do they *rush* on to war?

RECK, to emit vapor; to care or mind.

The soldier *recks* not his life?

WELTER, to wallow; to roll in blood.

Should the poor soldier be left to *welter* in his blood?

SLAUGHTER, to strike down; to make great havoc.

Did the armies *slaughter* each other?

WAVER, to move to and fro; to change in courage.

Should a soldier *waver?*

QUAIL, to sink away; to fall back and lose courage.

Does the coward *quail* in battle?

HARBOUR, to cover soldiers; to shelter in any way.

Should we *harbor* the criminal?

SPARE, to shut off; to keep from punishment or death.

Can man *spare* his enemy?

HURT, to dash at; to injure in any way.

Should children *hurt* each other?

COPE, to strive; to strive on equal terms.

Did America *cope* with England?

SHOOT, to throw out; to let fly an arrow.

Do men *shoot* balls?

DUB, to strike in naming; to strike with a sword in making a knight.

Does the king *dub* knights?

WAR, to urge against; to contend in battle.

FIGHT, to fetch a blow; to strive for victory in battle.

Is it wrong to *fight*?

HALT, to hold up; to stop on a march.

Do soldiers *halt* when they are tired?

DRILL, to turn; to exercise or train in arms.

Should the officer *drill* his men?

SHIELD, to cover; to protect from danger.

Does the soldier *shield* his country?

HEAD, to shoot or top; to lead or advance before.

Does the captain *head* his band?

BOAST, to use a bow; to praise oneself.

Do you like to *boast* of yourself?

COW, to make afraid; to awaken fear.

Does the keen look *cow* at times?

ONE HUNDRED AND FORTIETH STUDY.

ACTIONS OF THE TEACHER.

"IN every village marked with little spire,
Embowered in trees, and hardly known to fame,
There dwells, in lowly shed and mean attire,
A matron old, whom we schoolmistress name."

SHENSTONE.

TEACH, to point out; to give knowledge.

Is it easy to *teach* children?

SHOW, to hold to the eye; to present to view.

Does the teacher *show* her scholars how to do things?

FORM, to set; to give shape to.

Can you *form* a square?

READ, to drive out, as the voice; to utter written letters or words.

Should a teacher *read* well?

WRITE, to smear as with wax; to form letters and words.

Can your teacher *write* neatly?

RECKON, to count by balls; to count by figures.

Can you *reckon* quickly?

RULE, to direct; to govern and guide.

Should a teacher *rule* her pupils?

LEARN, to gather; to take up knowledge.

Does the good child *learn* well?

6*

ONE HUNDRED AND FORTY-FIRST STUDY.

ACTIONS OF THE DOCTOR.

> " PERMIT that I
> My little knowledge.with my country share,
> Till you the rich Asclepian stores unlock."
>
> DR. ARMSTRONG.

HEAL, to make sound; to cure sickness.

　　Can the doctor *heal* us?

BLEED, to cause to flow; to take away blood by opening a vein.

　　Should the doctor *bleed* her?

MIX, to stir.; to mingle things.

　　Does the doctor *mix* his medicines?

BRAY, to break in pieces; to pound in a mortar.

Do doctors *bray* medicines in a mortar?

BLISTER, to bloat; to raise the skin with a watery liquid.

　　Do doctors *blister* for fevers?

CUP, to use a cup to draw away blood.

　　Will the doctor *cup* for dropsy?

LEECH, to lessen; to treat with medicine and heal.

　　Do doctors *leech* the sick?

ONE HUNDRED AND FORTY-SECOND STUDY.

ACTIONS OF THE ARTIST.

> "O THOU sculptor, painter, poet!
> Take this lesson to thy heart;
> That is best which lieth nearest,
> Shape from that thy work of art."
>
> LONGFELLOW.

DRAW, to move over; to represent a picture by lines.

　　Can you *draw* objects?

SING, to strain; to give forth sweet sounds.

　　Do you like to *sing?*

PIPE, to make a sound by blowing; to play on a wind instrument.

　　Can the piper *pipe* on his pipes?

HARP, to play on a harp.

Do angels *harp* on golden harps?

GILD, to pay in gold; to cover with gold.

　　Does the artist *gild* frames?

DRAFT, to draw; to draw the shape of a thing.

　　Can the artist *draft?*

SKETCH, to cast forth; to draw an outline.

　　Does the artist *sketch* well?

BLEND, to mix; to mingle together.
Does the artist *blend* colors?

CARVE, to cut in; to shape any thing on wood or stone.
Do engravers *carve* on wood?

ONE HUNDRED AND FORTY-THIRD STUDY.

ACTIONS OF MINERALS.

"'I AM a pebble, and yield to none,'
Were the swelling words of a tiny stone!
'For I am as old as the big round earth?'"   GOULD.

SPURN,
GLISTEN, to shine; to shine with light.
Does gold *glisten?*
RUST, to become red; to become rusty.
Does iron *rust* in the air?

GLITTER, to sparkle; to sparkle with light.
Do diamonds *glitter?*
DWINDLE, to fall away; to become less.
Does lead *dwindle* away when melted?

ONE HUNDRED AND FORTY-FOURTH STUDY.

ACTIONS OF PLANTS.

"THE wind flower and the violet,
They perished long ago;
And the brier rose and the orchis died
Amid the summer's glow."   BRYANT.

GROW, to increase; to enlarge in size.
Do all plants *grow?*
EAR, to shoot; to form ears as corn.
Does the corn *ear* well?
LEAF, to shoot out; to put forth leaves.
Does the rose *leaf* in spring?
BLOSSOM, to open out; to put forth flowers.
Does the rose *blossom?*

SEED, to scatter; to grow and make seed.
Do farmers *seed* their ground?
WITHER, to become dry; to fade and lose its freshness.
Does the rose *wither* in autumn?
DROOP, to fall; to hang downward.
Does the lily of the valley *droop?*
CLOTHE, to cover; to cover over any thing.

Does our Creator *clothe* the trees with leaves?

FEED, to nourish; to supply food.
Does grass *feed* cattle?

DIE, to pass away; to lose life.
Does the rose *die*?

RUSTLE, to make quick, small sounds.
Do leaves *rustle*?

ONE HUNDRED AND FORTY-FIFTH STUDY.

ACTIONS OF DOMESTIC ANIMALS.

"THE low of herds
Blends with the rustling of the heavy grain."   BRYANT.

BELLOW, to belch out sound; to make a loud hollow noise.
Does the bull *bellow*?

LOW, to make a flat low sound; to make a low noise.
Does the cow *low*?

BLEAT, from the sound; to cry as sheep.
Does the sheep *bleat*?

BARK, from the sound; to make a sharp snapping noise.
Does the dog *bark*?

WORRY, to shake or tear; to harass or tear.
Does the dog *worry* his food?

WHINE, to squeak; to make a crying sound.
Does the dog *whine*?

FAWN, to crouch in joy; to seek favor or notice.
Does the dog *fawn* on his master?

NEIGH, from the sound; to make the sound of a horse.

Does the horse *neigh*?

BRAY, to make a grinding sound; to make a harsh loud sound.
Does the ass *bray*?

GRAZE, to eat grass; to feed on grass or herbage.
Do cattle *graze* in the field?

WAG, to shake; to move one way and the other, as the tail.
Does the dog *wag* his tail?

LICK, to rub; to draw the tongue over a thing.
Does the dog *lick* his master's hand?

CROW, from the sound; to make the noise of the cock.
Does the cock *crow*?

CLUCK, from the sound; to make the sound of the hen while hatching.
Does the hen *cluck*?

SLINK, to creep slily; to steal away.
Does puss *slink* behind the door?

ONE HUNDRED AND FORTY-SIXTH STUDY.

ACTIONS OF WILD ANIMALS.

"The wild boar sought his lair;
The wolf prowled through the wood;
The serpent hissed; nay, all the beasts
Gave signs of fear."

ROAR, to make a loud long noise.
Does the lion *roar?*

GRIN, to set the teeth; to open the mouth and set the teeth.
Does the wolf *grin?*

HISS, to make a hissing sound.
Does the black snake *hiss* when angry?

BRISTLE, to shoot up; to raise the hair.
Does the wild boar *bristle* when angry?

CREEP, to crawl; to move slowly.
Does the snake *creep?*

SPRING, to leap; to move with violence.

Does the lion *spring* on his prey?

TEAR, to waste; to separate with violence.
Does the tiger *tear* his food?

BURROW, to bore into; to make a hole in the earth.
Does the rabbit *burrow?*

CLIMB, to go up; to creep up a tree or rock.
Does the monkey *climb* trees?

LIMP, to walk as if lame.
Does the hare *limp* over the frozen grass?

ONE HUNDRED AND FORTY-SEVENTH STUDY.

ACTIONS OF WATER ANIMALS.

"SEEKEST thou the plashy brink
Of weedy lake, or marge of river wide,
Or where the rocking billows rise and sink
On the chafed ocean side?"   BRYANT.

CROAK, from the sound; to make a low hoarse noise.
Does the frog *croak?*

SUCK, to draw into; to imbibe or draw up a fluid.

Does the leech *suck* blood?

SWIM, to pass away; to move on or in water.
Do fish *swim* in water?

SCUTTLE, to make as a basket; to bore

a ship so as to be open like a basket.

Does the ship-worm *scuttle* ves-
sels?

SPAWN, to throw out; to throw out
eggs as a fish.

Do fish *spawn* once a year?

ONE HUNDRED AND FORTY-EIGHTH STUDY.

ACTIONS OF BIRDS.

" WITH storm-daring pinion, and sun-gazing eye,
The gray forest eagle is the king of the sky."　　　STREET.

FLY, to move with the wings; to
move through the air with wings.

Does the eagle *fly?*

HOP, to hobble; to spring on the
feet.

Does the robin *hop* merrily
about?

SWOOP, to carry off rapidly; to seize
on the wing.

Does the eagle *swoop* his prey?

FLUTTER, to waver: to move and flap
the wings.

Does the wounded bird *flutter?*

SCREAM, to cry out in fear; to utter
a loud shrill cry.

Does the eagle *scream* when
angry?

LAY, to put down; to bring forth as
eggs.

Do all birds *lay* eggs?

MOUNT, to go up; to soar on high.

Does the eagle *mount* on his
wings?

LIGHT, to lift; to get down as a bird
from on wing.

Does the bird *light* on the
branch?

ONE HUNDRED AND FORTY-NINTH STUDY.

ACTIONS OF THE EARTH.

" Earth that nourished thee shall claim
Thy growth, to be resolved to earth again."　BRYANT.

TURN, to wheel about; to move in a
circular course.

Does the earth *turn* on its axis?

WHIRL, to turn round quickly; to
roll rapidly.

Does water *whirl* in the whirl-
pool?

GLIDE, to move smoothly; to move
rapidly but smoothly.

FLOAT, to move as if on wing; to be
borne along on water or in the
air.

Do clouds *float* in the air?

QUAKE, to shake; to shake or tremble.

Does the earth sometimes *quake?*

TEEM, to bring forth; to swarm with life.

Does the earth *teem* with living things?

SWARM, to move as boiling water; to throng in crowds.

Does the air *swarm* with life?

SPROUT, to shoot; to spring forth as grass.

Does grass *sprout* up from the earth?

BEAR, to carry; to bring forth.

Does the earth *bear* grain?

ONE HUNDRED AND FIFTIETH STUDY.

ACTIONS OF BODIES OF WATER.

"AND why do the roaring ocean,
And the night-wind wild and bleak,
As they beat at the heart of the mother,
Drive the color from her cheek?" LONGFELLOW.

SWELL, to enlarge; to rise in billows.

Do the waves of the ocean *swell?*

FLOW, to move as water; to glide along as water.

Do streams *flow?*

FREEZE, to shrink; to harden into ice.

Does water *freeze?*

THAW, to flow; to melt what is frozen.

Does the sun *thaw* ice?

FLOOD, to flow over; to flow over its bounds.

Do rivers sometimes *flood* their banks?

DROWN, to draw over; to overwhelm in water.

Did the man *drown* his dog?

ONE HUNDRED AND FIFTY-FIRST STUDY.

ACTIONS OF THE HEAVENS.

"THE golden sun,
The planets, all the infinite host of heaven
Are shining on the sad abodes of death." BRYANT.

HANG, to waver; to suspend.

Do the clouds *hang* in the heavens?

WATER, to flow and wet; to pour out as rain.

Do the heavens *water* the earth?

SHADE, to cut off as light; to screen from the light.

Do clouds sometimes *shade* the sun?

DAZZLE, to make dizzy; to overpower with light.

Does the sun *dazzle* our eyes?

WHEEL, to turn about; to roll forward.

Does the bear *wheel* about the pole star?

RISE, to go up; to move or pass upwards.

Does the sun *rise* every morning?

SET, to drive; to pass below the horizon.

Does the sun *set* every evening?

TWINKLE, to wink; to shine tremblingly.

Do stars *twinkle?*

GLEAM, to shoot; to shoot forth rays.

Does the moon *gleam* in misty weather?

DRENCH, to drink; to soak as with rain.

Does rain *drench* the earth?

SPRINKLE, to scatter; to scatter as rain.

Do the clouds *sprinkle* rain?

DAWN, to become day; to open as the morning.

Does day *dawn* gently?

ONE HUNDRED AND FIFTY-SECOND STUDY.

ACTIONS OF GOD.

"OUR God, our Father, our eternal all!
Who made our spirits, who our bodies made,
Who made the heavens, who made the flowery land,
Who made all made, who orders governs all."   POLLOK.

MAKE, to form; to form into any shape.

Did God *make* the earth?

LAY, to throw down; to settle or fix.

Did God *lay* the foundations of the world?

REAR, to raise up; to raise or build.

Did God *rear* the earth?

FIX, to fasten; to make firm.

Did God *fix* the earth in its place?

HOLD, to strain; to bind fast, or together.

Does God *hold* the sea in the hollow of his hand?

KEEP, to thrust; to hold or preserve.

Does God *keep* us from harm?

CURSE, to bring evil upon one.

Does God *curse* the wicked?

BLESS, to make happy; to confer good on one.

Does God *bless* the good?

ATONE, to make one; to satisfy for sin.

Should we *atone* for our sins?

CHAPTER XIII.

EVENTS.

EVENTS OF THE HOUSEHOLD.

THE death of children in early life is a sad event; the blight of buds of promise.

> "I saw the nursery windows
> Wide open to the air;
> But the faces of the children,
> They were no longer there." LONGFELLOW.

WED, to pledge love; to unite in marriage.

Do men and women *wed* each other ?

WEDDING, a pledging of love; a marriage.

Did you attend the *wedding* ?

BIRTH, a bringing forth; coming into life.

Do you watch the *birth* of the flowers ?

WORK, what is done by effort; labor of any kind.

Should all men *work* ?

PLAY, a throwing off work; sport or amusement.

Do children like *play* ?

SLEEP, a loosening; rest by suspending the powers of body and mind.

Do children *sleep* sweetly ?

ONE HUNDRED AND FIFTY-THIRD STUDY.

EVENTS IN THE OCCUPATIONS OF MAN.

> "So many hours must I tend my flock;
> So many hours must I take my rest;
> So many hours must I contemplate." SHAKSPEARE.

SEED-TIME, time of sowing; the season for sowing.

Is spring the *seed-time* of the year ?

HARVEST, the food part of the year; the season for gathering the crops.

Is August a *harvest* month ?

SOWING, a scattering; the art of seeding a field.

Is *sowing* a toilsome work ?

BLIGHT, a scurf; a disease that nips plants or grain.

Does the farmer dread the *blight?*

MILDEW, honey-dew; a white coating on plants.

Does *mildew* injure plants?

SHIPWRECK, ship-breaking; the casting away of a ship.

Is a *shipwreck* a dreadful thing?

FALL, a driving; the act of dropping from a high place.

Does snow *fall* to the earth?

WOUND, a thrust; a hurt of any kind.

Is a *wound* painful?

RUST, red; a disease in grain.

Does *rust* injure wheat?

BEGINNING, a going in; the first of any thing.

Did God create the earth in the *beginning?*

LOSS, a parting; a ceasing to possess something.

Do we mourn the *loss* of our friends?

FIRE, a raging; the burning of any thing.

Is *fire* useful?

ONE HUNDRED AND FIFTY-FOURTH STUDY.

EVENTS OF THE EARTH.

"Now that winter's gone, the earth hath lost
  Her snow-white robes, and now no more the frost
  Candies the grass, or calls an icy cream
  Upon the silver lake."

                        CAREW.

COLD, a blowing; the want of heat.

Is winter *cold?*

HEAT, fire; a state of warmth.

Does the fire give out *heat?*

DAY, opening; the time when the sun is with us.

Does the sun shine during the *day?*

NIGHT, black; the time when the sun is absent.

Does the moon shine at *night?*

SPRING, a shooting; the season of buds.

Is *spring* pleasant?

SUMMER, hot or sun time; the flowering of the earth.

Do roses bloom in *summer?*

FALL, a dropping; the time of decay

Is *fall* dreary?

WINTER, windy time; the sleep of the earth.

Does snow fall in *winter?*

WIND, a moving; the air in motion.

Do you like to hear the *wind?*

BLAST, a striking; a sudden gust of wind.

Did you hear the *blast?*

BREEZE, a moving; a gentle blow of air.

Is a *breeze* pleasant?

STORM, a raging; a strong wind and rain.

Is a *storm* often fearful?

SHOWER, a shaking; a fall of rain.

Does a *shower* do good!

HAIL, a driving; a fall of frozen rain.

Does *hail* do any harm!

SNOW, a glistening; a fall of frozen vapor.

Is *snow* white!

ICE, what is firm; water frozen solid.

Is *ice* clear!

FROST, a shining; frozen mist or fog.

Is *frost* a pleasing thing!

MIST, what mixes; water falling in very small drops.

Is *mist* gloomy!

DEW, what gleams; moisture in the air made into drops.

Is *dew* sparkling!

FLOOD, a rushing; a great flow of water.

Do *floods* occur in spring!

WAVE, a going to and fro; a moving swell of water.

Does the wind make *waves!*

TIDE, a hopping; the rise and fall of the waters of the sea.

Does the moon make the *tide!*

LAND-SLIP, a moving of land; a slide of land.

Does a *land-slip* destroy any thing!

SPRING, a leaping; a boiling up of water.

Is a *spring* beautiful!

FALL, a throwing; a descent of water.

Is a *fall* of water a fine sight!

ONE HUNDRED AND FIFTY-FIFTH STUDY.

EVENTS IN THE HEAVENS.

"THE sky is changed! and such a change! O night,
And storm and darkness, ye are wondrous strong.
From peak to peak the rattling crags among
Leaps the live thunder."

BYRON.

LIGHT, a darting forth; that by which we see.

Is *light* pleasing to the eye!

TWILIGHT, doubtful light; light before the rising and setting of the sun.

Is *twilight* the time for thought!

CLOUD, a mass; a mass of visible vapor.

Does the *cloud* sail in the air!

DAWN, opening; the break of day.

Is the *dawn* the time to rise!

THUNDER, a clashing; the sound that follows lightning.

Is *thunder* a fearful thing!

LIGHTNING, a flashing; a flash of light before a thunder-clap.

Is *lightning* a strong thing!

SUNRISE, a going of the sun; the first appearance of the sun.

Is *sunrise* beautiful!

SUNSET, a sinking of the sun; the going down of the sun.

Is a *sunset* glorious!

RAINBOW, an arch of colors made by the sun shining on rain.

Is a *rainbow* a lovely sight!

RAIN, what flows; falling drops of water.

Is *rain* useful to the farmer!

ONE HUNDRED AND FIFTY-SIXTH STUDY.

EVENTS OF GOD.

"THE spacious firmament on high,
With all the blue ethereal sky,
And spangled heavens, a shining frame,
Their great Original proclaim."   ADDISON.

EARTH, dust; the place on which plants, animals and man live.

Is the *earth* our world?

HEAVEN, lifted up; the sky or place round the earth.

Is *heaven* above the earth?

SUN, the shiner; the body that lights the earth by day.

Is the *sun* bright?

MOON, what directs; the body that lights the earth by night.

Do you like to see the *moon?*

STAR, what steers; a bright body that sparkles at night in the sky.

Is a *star* a world.

WORLD, round; the earth, or the universe.

Is the earth called the *world?*

MAN, strong; the race of thinking beings to which we belong; God's image on earth.

Is *man* a thinking being?

FALL, a casting down; the ruin of God's image in man by sin.

Did Adam *fall* by sin?

GOSPEL, good-speaking; good news from God to man.

Is the *gospel* news about Christ?

DAYSMAN, the strength of day; one who unites parties, as sinful man and offended God.

Is Christ our *daysman?*

PEACE, pressed down; rest from every thing that troubles.

Does Christ give *peace?*

ONE HUNDRED AND FIFTY-SEVENTH STUDY.

LAST THINGS.

"THUS have I sung beyond thy first request,
Rolling my numbers o'er the track of man,
The world at dawn, at midday, and decline;
Time gone, the righteous saved, the wicked damned,
And God's eternal government approved."   POLLOK.

END, a point; the close or last of any thing.

Is death the *end* of life on earth !

DEATH, a falling away; the end of life on earth.

Is *death* sometimes fearful !

GRAVE, a place dry; the place of the dead.

Is the *grave* the last resting-place of the body !

COURT, a circuit; a place of justice.

- Is the *court* of heaven to be entered !

DOOM, judgment; sentence or fixed state of man.

Is the *doom* of man known after death !

HELL, a covered place; the abode of the wicked.

Is there a *hell* !

HEAVEN, lifted up; the high abode; the home of God, angels, and saints.

Do holy persons go to *heaven* !

ONE HUNDRED AND FIFTY-EIGHTH STUDY.

THE END OF THE SECOND PART.

THE second part of the HAND-BOOK OF ANGLO-SAXON ROOT-WORDS is ended. We began it with the words of HOME, and closed it with the words of LAST THINGS.

Between these two points there is a wide space. We have passed over it THREE TIMES. The FIRST TIME we noticed the things lying between home and heaven, and gathered up their NAMES. Thus, *home, house,* under the HEAD, Home. We did more than this. We learned what they meant, when the *Saxons* first used them; and also what they mean now with us. Thus, *home,* a cover, the place where one lives.

The SECOND TIME we marked the QUALITIES of things lying between home and heaven, and picked up the WORDS that stand for them. Thus, under home, we got *sweet, dear.*

The THIRD TIME, we noticed the ACTIONS of things lying between home and heaven, and learned the words that stand for them.   Thus, under the senses, we got the words, *look, hear, smell, feel.*

In this way, the mind grows in learning words and joining them with things.   Thus, your mind grows.   Already you possess over ONE THOUSAND root-words, and are able to point out their meanings, and use them in speech.   These are like seeds.   They will produce other words.   Some TWENTY THOUSAND form their great offspring.

THIRD PART.

THE BEGINNINGS OF THE ROOT-WORDS.

THE BEGINNINGS OF THE ROOT-WORDS.

CHAPTER I.

THE BEGINNING OF WORDS.

WORDS have a beginning. We propose to seek it in the human body, the great instrument from which the soul awakens words.

ONE HUNDRED AND FIFTY-NINTH STUDY.

WORDS.

WORDS are now well-known things. Already you know over *one thousand.* What are they?

Words are the sounds that pass from the lips. They are made on the organ of speech.

ONE HUNDRED AND SIXTIETH STUDY.

THE ORGAN OF SPEECH.

THE organ of speech is the instrument by which we speak. It is made up of the following parts: the *lips, teeth, tongue, palate* and *throat.*

7

On this organ we speak and sing. *It is the source of words.*
All words are formed on the organ of speech.

ONE HUNDRED AND SIXTY-FIRST STUDY.

THE BODY AND WORDS.

THE body, as well as the organ of speech, has something
to do with making words. Every part of the body helps
us to make them. The lips give us *sip* and *sup*, the hands
handle, *haft*, *hold*, and the feet *step*, *walk*, *stand*.

ONE HUNDRED AND SIXTY-SECOND STUDY.

THE WORLD AND WORDS.

THE world also has something to do with making words.
Every thing without us helps us to them. The mother's
voice first gave us the words, *pa* and *ma*. Servants, brothers
and sisters helped us to others—*dog*, *cat*, *chick*. The fire led
us to pick up *burn*, *hot*. The dog helped us to *bow-wow*, and
the cat to *mew;* the hen to *cluck* and *cackle*, and the cow
to *low* and *moo*.

ONE HUNDRED AND SIXTY-THIRD STUDY.

THE SOUL AND WORDS.

THE soul has more to do with making words than every
thing else. The organ of voice and body are the instrument on which it makes them. The world helps it to do
so. Do you understand this?

I will make it plain. I take a cup of tea and suck in a
little of it with my lips. You hear the sound *sip*, and say,

I *sip* my tea. I tell you something that makes you very happy. You strike your hands together, and I hear the sound *clap*, and say you *clap* me. So the soul picks up words from all things.

ONE HUNDRED AND SIXTY-FOURTH STUDY.

THE BEGINNINGS OF WORDS.

ALL words came forth from the lips, but all words did not begin there. Some of them began in the motions of the hands, others in the action of the feet; and some in breathing. Some words began in the noise made by animals; others in the growth of flowers and the beams of the sun. In these and other things, we have the beginnings of words.

If we take now the THOUSAND words we have learned, and look at them in their beginnings, we will see clearly what they mean. We will find *clasp, finger, grope* and *feel* beginning with the hands: *look, see, hear, taste,* with the senses. Thus, we shall trace words up to their beginnings, as we trace streams up to their springs.

ONE HUNDRED AND SIXTY-FIFTH STUDY.

NATURAL HISTORY OF WORDS.

WORDS, like every thing else, have a beginning and a growth. This is their history.

All the words that we use, form one family. Some of them are older than others. Thus *red* and *yellow* are older than *brown* or *gray*. They first pleased us, and were first used.

Some of them have their beginnings in one part of the body and some in another. The feet, for instance, give us *foot, step, steep, mount ;* the hand helps us to such words as *hand, handle, take, hold.*

We are now ready to look at the *one thousand Anglo-Saxon root-words in their beginnings.* In doing this, one simple rule will be our guide—WORDS WILL BE FOUND UNDER THE PARTS OF THE BODY, OR THAT WHICH PUTS THE BODY IN ACTION.

CHAPTER II.

THE HUMAN BODY.

THE human body is the instrument on which the soul forms words.

ONE HUNDRED AND SIXTY-SIXTH STUDY.

THE ORGAN OF SPEECH.

THE ORGAN OF SPEECH IS THE FOUNT OF WORDS.

SPEECH, speak, lisp, word, song, sing, lip, mouth, tongue, pipe, answer, mourn, reck, chide, say, bid, bequeath, read, gospel.

ONE HUNDRED AND SIXTY-SEVENTH STUDY.

THE SENSE OF HEARING.

THE organ of speech would be useless without this sense. It guides speech. The following words mostly mark SOUND.

Sound, ear, hear, hearing, clock, tick, bell, gong, cow, bullock, swine, frog, owl, crow, lark, dove, cuckoo, goose, gander, gosling, winter, hare, slumber, snore, weep, hearken, listen, list, moan, craze, stun, smack, scream, sup, sip, singe, dun, rustle, bellow, low, bleat, bark, whine, greet, neigh, bray, crow, cluck, roar, hiss, croak, thunder.·

ONE HUNDRED AND SIXTY-EIGHTH STUDY.

THE SENSE OF SEEING.

THIS sense helps us to some words. It aids the organ of speech in getting those words that mark COLOR.

Red, yellow, blue, white, black, dark, wan, green, brown, gray, dun, coal, flint, gold, gall, silver, glass, brass, brimstone, ash, sallow, radish, ruddy, swan, fair, foam, welkin, roach, tidy, blank, bright, look, blink, seek, stare, dye, neal, bleach, glaze, brand, reck, show, glisten, rust, glitter, twinkle, snow, frost, dew, lightning.

ONE HUNDRED AND SIXTY-NINTH STUDY.

THE SENSE OF TASTE.

THIS sense helps us to words that mark the flavor of things.

Sweet, sour, tart, salt, rue, sorrel, sloe, acid, prove.

ONE HUNDRED AND SEVENTIETH STUDY.

THE SENSE OF SMELL.

THIS sense helps us to words that mark ODORS.
Smell, smelling, fennel, stench, stink.

THE SENSE OF TOUCH.

THIS sense aids the organ of speech in forming a large class of words. They mark feelings of what is WARM, COLD, EVEN, ROUGH.

Touch, warm, hot, cold, cool, even, rough, end, rye, bere, barley, harp, brier, thorn, bramble, shrub, nettle, thistle, spur, pen, desk, boar, lobster, trout, wet, mead, meadow, clay, lime, fir, oil, south, summer, wide, broad, narrow, rim, boat, bellows, mound, brow, neck, nape, back, pimple, heel, ankle, blain, knee, thigh, hip, dough, loaf, bread, nose, chin, kernel, pith, lump, hate, feud, fiend, foe, shabby, raw, mild, keen, sharp, pain, smooth, harvest, whet, heat, melt, blister, cold, wither.

ONE HUNDRED AND SEVENTY-SECOND STUDY.

THE HANDS.

THE *use* of the hand helps us to a large class of words.

Hand, handle, haft, finger, fist, hold, sleeve, rake, thresh, reap, mow, sow, plough, hunt, fish, hook, mill, smith, weave, buy, sell, spin, hammer, crib, herd, axe, saw, sledge, hoe, sickle, scythe, whip, pin, loom, yarn, silk, web, slaie, woof, warp, ladle, beetle, nave, rope, anvil, tongs, milk, butter, cup, wheat, meal, helmet, tow, span, fathom, yard, dart, seed, heath, mistletoe, pitch, leech, knife, thin, thick, haggard, raven, claw, cliff, dell, shore, parsnep, beat, twist, comb, cheapen, wrest, ward, hand, dub, fight, brittle, creep, grope, gripe, write, mise, bray, blend, lick, climb, grapple, clap, clutch, clip, strike, stroke, reach, box, have, like, knead, churn, milk, wring, slay, throw, spear, seed, reap, rake, thresh, gather, earn, sunder, saw, hew, cleave, drill.

ONE HUNDRED AND SEVENTY-THIRD STUDY.

THE FEET.

THE use of the feet furnish us with some words.

Foot, step, slip, steep, steeple, trap, road, mount, cloven, trip, ford, run, full, halt, slink, creep, spring, limp, hop, mount, rise.

ONE HUNDRED AND SEVENTY-FOURTH STUDY.

THE MUSCLES.

. THE muscles are bundles of fibres. They act by *drawing* and *stretching*. In this way they move the body, or any part of it.. Their *use* supplies us with a very large class of words, in addition to those under the *organ of speech, hands* and *feet.*

1. *Words that mark* GOING *or* MOVING. Go, do, bear, spring, out, in, ague, mood, boil, cook, well, monger, watch, bridge, bier, cart, wagon, wheel, barrow, sail, sling, court, car, cradle, goat, lamb, deer, roe, ape, whale, flea, fowl, fresh, fickle, wild, ready, bold, quick, merry, wriggle, begin, glide, wonder, gad, shun, turn, wend, waver, wag, turn, whirl, beginning, wave, fish.

2. *Words that mark* DRAWING *or* TAKING. Last, drag, dray, seine, ladder, teach, mind, moon, star, chuze, elephant, snake, worm, snail, dread, tough, sigh, drink, lead, pull, spin, cow, suck, freeze, drench.

3. *Words that mark* STRETCHING *or* GIVING. Stretch, right, reach, play, pain, pang, ache, sick, belt, bed, roof, sheet, war, fight, work, pan, dish, spade, board, rack, side, wing, keel, reed, spindle, ridge, bay, hall, cock, chicken, hen, hound, late, earnest, early, better, best, hope, feel, feeling, rank, greedy, gape, look, stare, wish, send, tie, give, work, mete, lie, cope, war.

4. *Words that mark* THRUSTING *or* SHOOTING. Thrust, shoot, shot, spasm, shooting, rod, arrow, spike, plough, shovel, stuff, tooth, sprout, toe, ear, willow, ram, buck, horse, peak, ditch, kiln, keep, fire, sneeze, spit, laugh, loath, break, hunt, wound, dig, shovel, bore, hurt, head, shoot, bristle, hail.

5. *Words that mark* FIRM *or* STRONG, RESISTING. Hard, soft, strong, strength, body, heart, fist, knuckle, lock, latch, post, stem, stove, mast, hasp, key, besom, iron, saddle, starch, stag, might, stark, stony, hemp, oak, holly, clam, lobster, steady, doughty, kind, king, stubborn, good, will, law, stand, stall, stool, hoof, dam, target, furze, horn, wool, binding, bow, elbow, cup, door, gate, nostril, sap, ice, mouth, fan, acre, fold, crafty, cunning, stern.

6. *Words that mark* LIFTING *or* PRESSING DOWN. Lift, light, head, high, leaf, east, eastern, west, open, low, night, noon, peace, bolster, pillow, sill, wharf, ground, field, wright, heavy, ballast, felt, shoal, load, flock, spare, glad, blithe, joy, glee, sorrow, fear, cap, tippet, foul, dead, many, level, sit, lie, rise, nap, lift, brook, open, weary, weave, quell, lay, fall, nod.

7. *Words that denote* LOOSENING *or* RESTING. · Rest, sleep, creed, truth, love, sin, laugh, smile, tear, blood, water, wash, flax, liquor, tar, lank, wan, evening, old, idle, slow, swoon, spill, quail, droop

ONE HUNDRED AND SEVENTY-FIFTH STUDY.

THE ORGAN OF BREATHING.

THE *use* of the organ of breathing helps us to some words. Breathe, breath, soul, ghost, life, live.

ONE HUNDRED AND SEVENTY-SIXTH STUDY.

THE COVERING OF THE BODY.

THE *need* of covering or defending the body helps us to a useful group of words.

Cloth, clothing, mantle, hat, glove, hose, shoe, shroud, sheet, home, house, hut, hovel, hamlet, shed, cot, cottage, hall, town, skin, hide, bark, maple, shield, cap, shoulder, pride, pretty, bury, clothe, deck, screen, swaddle, stable, pen, roof, board, spare, shield, wallow.

ONE HUNDRED AND SEVENTY-SEVENTH STUDY.

FOOD.

FOOD and its use help us to some words.

Food, feed, meat, oats, ham, farm, poppy, dine, craw, carve, soak, swoop.

CHAPTER III.

MAN.

MAN is a social being, and as such furnishes us with many words.

7*

ONE HUNDRED AND SEVENTY-EIGHTH STUDY.

MAN.

MAN, in his *form.* and *growth* and conditions of life, gives us some words.

Man, woman, queen, knight, swain, boor, bear, ail, hallow, yawn, bide, rest, rouse, heal, quake, death, wise, wisdom, wicked.

ONE HUNDRED AND SEVENTY-NINTH STUDY.

THE HOUSEHOLD.

THE *household* is the first form of society, and gives a rich class of words.

Husband, wife, father, mother, child, son, daughter, brother, sister, bairn, kin, kindred, steward, kiss, ask, meet, scorch, clean, sweep, wash, wipe, quench, foster, warm, rinse, rear, dear, darling.

ONE HUNDRED AND EIGHTIETH STUDY.

SOCIETY.

DIFFERENT forms of society branch out from the household. The *church* and *state* are the chief, and supply some words.

Fellow, neighbor, guest, yeoman, henchman, hireling, hire, friend, elder, bishop, sheriff, canon, monk, nun, provost, ruler, priest, worship, bow, taunt, bet, gain, bargain, harbor, loss.

ONE HUNDRED AND EIGHTY-FIRST STUDY.

BUSINESS OF MAN.

THE business or occupations of man furnish some words, the names of some instruments and works.

Box, chest, deck, weir, ripe, swear, cook, bake, grind, knit, whittle, hem, sew, fish, steer, row, toil, boil, wreck, sail, swamp, farm, till, weed, mow, fan, hire, frame, build, buy, store, sell, boast, cup, gild, rear, fix.

CHAPTER IV.

THE WORLD.

THE earth and the heavens act upon the body of man, and help us to the names of bodies and their qualities.

ONE HUNDRED AND EIGHTY-SECOND STUDY.

THE EARTH.

THE *land, water, minerals, plants* and *animals* of the earth help us to many words.

1. EARTH.—Heath, heathen, earth, hearth, island.
2. LAND.—Land, hill, sward, ledge.
3. WATER.—Water, sea, stream, swift, flow, thaw, flood, drown, tide, bay, creek, sound.
4. MINERALS.—Lead, steel, sand.
5. PLANTS.—Book, limb, barn, grass, grain, grow, flay, fir, linden, yew, ivy, madder, leaf, blossom, blight, mildew.
6. ANIMALS.—Bird, nail, claw, scale, rampant, tame, stray, skin, ride, swim, rush, welter, graze, lick, worry, grin, tear, fly, teem, flutter, swarm, bean.

ONE HUNDRED AND EIGHTY-THIRD STUDY.

THE HEAVENS.

THE heavens, and what they contain, supply us with some words.

Heaven, sun, light, ray, day, dawn, morn, morning, daisy, Sunday, Monday, Thursday, Friday, Saturday, twilight, weather, dazzle, gleam, sprinkle, shade, set, blast, breeze, storm, shower, cloud.

ONE HUNDRED AND EIGHTY-FOURTH STUDY.

FORM.

THE *shapes* of things act upon our senses, and are named.
Shape, ship, shop, shilling, rib, form, draw, draft, sketch, world.

ONE HUNDRED AND EIGHTY-FIFTH STUDY.

QUANTITY.

THE *size* or dimensions of things acts upon our senses, and aids us in forming some words.

Size, long, length, side, end, tall, short, thumb, liver, board, broad, spade, lungs, farthing, boot, some, all, great, part, weigh, deal, leech, dwindle, swell.

ONE HUNDRED AND EIGHTY-SIXTH STUDY.

PLACE.

THE *places* of things are brought into notice by the things, and help us to some words.

Room, stead, stern, oar, pier, harbor, through, land, hell, grave.

ONE HUNDRED AND EIGHTY-SEVENTH STUDY.

TIME.

THE things without us are active, and as one thing succeeds another, we get the notion of time—get it from SUCCESSION.

Time, winter, summer, watch.

ONE HUNDRED AND EIGHTY-EIGHTH STUDY.

RELATIONS OF THINGS IN PLACE AND TIME.

THESE are noticed, and give us some words.

In, out, to, of, from, towards, by, with, near, about, around, above, under, down, up, for, through, first, prime.

ONE HUNDRED AND EIGHTY-NINTH STUDY.

CONNECTIONS OF THINGS IN PLACE AND TIME.

WE observe these, and get from this quarter some words.

And, but, if, though, or, as, so, that, lest, still, till, since, then, else, yet, than.

CHAPTER V.

THE SOUL AND GOD.

THE body and the world could not aid the organ of speech to form words without the soul and God.

ONE HUNDRED AND NINETIETH STUDY.

THE SOUL.

THE soul is the fount of all words. The organ of speech and the body are only its instruments. The world is the material.

Like, little, true, believe, think, know, heed, doom, teach, learn, think, thought, same, like.

ONE HUNDRED AND NINETY-FIRST STUDY.

GOD.

GOD is the Creator of *words* as well as works. He made the soul to speak. He taught man some words, and formed the soul, so as to make others for herself as they were needed.

Make, bless, curse, daysman, atone.

CHAPTER VI.

THE END OF THE HAND-BOOK OF ANGLO-SAXON ROOT-WORDS.

THE end of a good book is better than its beginning. It adds something to our knowledge.

Let us see what the *Hand-Book of Anglo-Saxon Root-words* has added. It is wise to look back, and gather up all we have seen and learned by the way.

FIRST PART.

THE FIRST·PART led us to a knowledge of words. We learned much about spoken and written words, and the ways of writing and spelling them. Letters, sounds and speech were explained.

SECOND PART.

The Second Part made us master of *one thousand root-words*. We began at home, and went out over all the things lying between home and heaven, and *named them;* learned the first and common meanings of these names, and used them in sentences. We returned, and went forth the second time over the same things, and named their *qualities.* Again, we returned, and went forth the third time over the same things, and named their *actions.*

THIRD PART.

The Third Part led us to the BEGINNINGS of these *one thousand root-words.* We saw them come forth from the lips. The organ of speech is the instrument of words. The body and all its parts aid this organ, and help it to words. So does the world. The *soul* uses all these, and is the fount of all words. God is their maker in forming the soul for speech, and teaching man to speak.

LaVergne, TN USA
19 November 2009

164702LV00007B/223/A